# Engaging Researchers with Data Management

## The Cookbook

*Connie Clare, Maria Cruz,*
*Elli Papadopoulou, James Savage,*
*Marta Teperek, Yan Wang, Iza Witkowska,*
*and Joanne Yeomans*

All external links were active at the time of publication unless otherwise stated and have been archived via the Internet Archive Wayback Machine at https://archive.org/web

Updated digital material and resources associated with this volume are available at https://doi.org/10.11647/OBP.0185#resources

# Contents

# Acknowledgements


We would like to thank Alastair Dunning, Head of Research Data Services at TU Delft Library for sponsoring the book sprint.

We would also like to thank:

**Alastair Dunning**, Head of Research Data Services, TU Delft Library;

**Raman Ganguly**, University of Vienna, Central Computer Centre;

**Lauren Cadwallader**, Deputy Manager of Scholarly Communication (Research Data Management), Cambridge University Library;

**Hilary Hanahoe**, Secretary-General, Research Data Alliance;

**Joeri Both**, Head of Research Support, Vrije Universiteit Amsterdam;

**Laurents Sesink**, Head of Centre for Digital Scholarship, Leiden University Libraries;

**Joshua Finnell**, Associate Professor in the University Libraries, Colgate University Research Council, Colgate University; and

**Martine Pronk**, Academic Services Department Manager, and Iza Witkowska, Research Data Consultant, Utrecht University Library;

for contributing to the publishing costs of the book.

# Foreword

Research data management is no longer a new or unknown concept for today's researchers, but nonetheless it can be intimidating. Many universities, institutes, organisations, and funding agencies have guidelines, mandates, and even policies around data management. But that does not make the task any less daunting; indeed it often adds a complicated layer of work and effort to data-producing research activities. Domain- and discipline-specific data comes in all sizes and forms, so specialised information is required to facilitate correct research data management. In addition, in recent years the very important and highly popular 'FAIR' principles[1] have been brought into the picture.

Fig. I. Hilary Hanahoe, Secretary-General, Research Data Alliance, CC BY 4.0.

*Engaging Researchers with Data Management: The Cookbook* has been compiled and edited by experts from the Research Data Alliance (RDA) to support anyone who helps researchers to understand and navigate their way around research

1 Mark D. Wilkinson et al., 'The FAIR Guiding Principles for scientific data management and stewardship', *Scientific Data* 3:160018 (2016), https://doi.org/10.1038/sdata.2016.18

data management and to find solutions. The RDA[2] is an international forum building social and technical bridges to enable the sharing and re-use of research data. It offers open solutions to multiple stakeholders through outputs developed by focused Working Groups and Interest Groups. These groups are formed by volunteer experts from around the world and draw members from academia, the private sector and government. This publication is one such output.

The Libraries for Research Data Interest Group[3] is one of over 85 RDA groups and has already produced the highly successful *23 Things: Libraries for Research Data*.[4] This output is an overview of the practical, free, online resources and tools that you can begin using today to incorporate research data management into your practice of librarianship. The document is available in twelve languages and a 23 Things programme has been created and adapted into more than six domain-specific scenarios.

The *Cookbook* is another wonderful output from this Interest Group and a concrete example of volunteer effort within the RDA community, as well as the continued contribution of the Libraries for Research Data Interest Group to RDA and the community at large.

Collaboration, cooperation and co-creation are the hallmarks of the RDA and the *Cookbook* team's activities. I am very grateful to each and every member of the large team of editors, authors, illustrators and case-study contributors for their effort and expertise.

I sincerely hope that you, the readers, will be inspired and feel more engaged after reading this publication and, if you are a researcher, will join the cohort of colleagues who believe that research data management is not only less daunting than is generally believed, but also a win-win for your career.

Hilary Hanahoe
Secretary-General, Research Data Alliance

---

2 Research Data Alliance, https://www.rd-alliance.org/

3 Libraries for Research Data Interest Group, https://www.rd-alliance.org/groups/libraries-research-data.html

4 Research Data Alliance, *23 Things: Libraries For Research Data*, https://www.rd-alliance.org/group/libraries-research-data-ig/outcomes/23-things-libraries-research-data-supporting-output

data
case
book
engage
RDM
institution
selection
study
survey
cases
good
innovative
used
asked
final
Data
Book
list
might
five
key
initiative
interviews
focus
help
interest
sprint
lists
make
senior
one
find
ease
read
select
writers
shared
based
will
also
first
hope
cost
may
interested
can
new
context
open
want

# I. Introduction

Good Research Data Management (RDM) is a key component of research integrity and reproducible research, and its value is increasingly emphasised by funding bodies, governments, and research institutions. However, discussions about data management and sharing are often limited to librarians, data professionals, and researchers who are already passionate about data stewardship and open science. In order to implement good RDM practice throughout research communities a cultural shift is necessary, and effective engagement with researchers, who are the main data producers and re-users, is essential for this shift to happen.

## What Is this Book About?

This book contains 24 RDM case studies, each describing an innovative activity used by a research institution to engage with its researchers about research data. These case studies, collected from research institutions worldwide, illustrate the diversity of feasible initiatives that could be implemented in other institutional settings.

The aim of this book is to inspire and inform those responsible for RDM using activities that have already been implemented and reflected upon elsewhere, and to help drive overall cultural change towards better data management. Our focus is not on what constitutes good research data management, but rather how it can be effectively communicated to the research community.


https://doi.org/10.11647/OBP.0185.24

## Who Is this Book For?

This book has been written for anyone interested in RDM, or good research practice more generally. It will be particularly useful to those interested in how to effectively engage with researchers about research data management. This might include librarians, data managers, data stewards, archivists, members of ICT (Information and Communication Technology) departments, colleagues from legal and financial support, faculty management, senior executives at institutions, funders, policymakers, publishers, members of the commercial sector, and researchers at any career stage who want to change practices among their peers. In short, if you have read this far, then this book is for you.

## Why Read this Book?

We hope that reading this book will:

- inspire you to implement new activities to engage with researchers about research data;
- help you find the activities most suitable for your institutional setting (according to size, research profile, resources available for data management, target audience, etc.);
- inform you about the ease of implementing each case, identifying the specific challenges associated with them and possible tips to overcome these;
- give you a general overview of what other institutions around the world do to engage their researchers with research data;
- provide you with tangible suggestions for actions that you could present to senior management at your institution;
- stimulate collaboration. We hope that reading our case studies and learning about the initiatives adopted by contributing institutions will lead to new connections and cooperation.

## How Should I Read the Book?

However you want! We designed this book with a diverse audience in mind, and while some might be keen to read everything from beginning to end, others may decide to focus on a selection of the most relevant chapters or case studies. All of our case studies have been carefully selected for your interest, however, you might find our 'How to Use This Cookbook' infographic helpful to navigate the cases of most interest to you. This book is analogous to a cookbook in the sense that it presents each individual case study in a similar format to that of a recipe. Each case study contains a list of 'key ingredients', that is, the institutional context and key elements required to successfully implement the initiative, as judged by the people directly involved. For example, information on the number of researchers involved, the target audience, the cost and ease of its implementation are presented in comprehensible, visual manner so that the reader can easily understand and compare case studies.

## How Did this Book Come About?

There are many interesting initiatives utilised by research institutions all over the world to effectively engage with their research communities about research data. Typically, those interested in RDM support and engagement learn about these diverse activities at conferences, by going to a talk from someone who implemented such an initiative and/or discussing it in person. In addition, some RDM units and institutional libraries may have blogs that report their ongoing activities, and well-connected individuals may pick up useful information directly through their networks. . But is this really the most effective way to share good practice? What about those who cannot attend conferences, or those who are just starting with RDM and don't yet have established connections or know where to look online for more information? How do they get started?

With these concerns in mind, the authors, together with members of Research Data Alliance[1] (and the Libraries for Research Data Interest Group[2] in particular) decided to collect information from various institutions worldwide on how they engage researchers about managing their research data. The goal was to make this body of knowledge about good practice more readily available by collecting it into a book that

1 Research Data Alliance, https://www.rd-alliance.org/

2 Libraries for Research Data Interest Group, https://www.rd-alliance.org/groups/libraries-research-data.html

would be more discoverable and accessible to the wider community of research data supporters. Our goal was to make it as easy as possible for others to get started supporting good practice in RDM, and rather than reinventing the wheel, facilitate the adoption and adaptation of existing methods from similar institutional settings. We hope you find this book as interesting to read, as we found collecting the information and putting it all together.[3]

3 A blog post about the book sprint during which we wrote the *Cookbook* is available online: Connie Clare, 'Book Sprint Success: A Team Writing Exercise for the Win', 23 July 2019, https://www.rd-alliance.org/blogs/book-sprint-success-team-writing-exercise-win.html

# II. Methodology

The aim of the project 'Research Engagement with Data Management' was to collect case studies from different organisations around the globe that focus on how to engage with the research community about research data management. By asking various questions about the models used and also about the organisational context, we created a useful resource for organisations that are looking to increase their engagement with their research communities.

In order to achieve this, we first designed and sent out a survey 'Researcher Engagement with Data Management: What Works?' to 60 funders, 80 scientific institutions, and 28 relevant mailing lists worldwide, as well as social media channels including blogs and Twitter. The survey was open from 18 January until 14 February 2019, and is available through Zenodo.[4]

Respondents were asked to think about which of their methods of researcher engagement would be of interest to other organisations. Each respondent was encouraged to mention as many initiatives used to engage researchers as they thought relevant, and to fill in the survey separately for each initiative. In addition, they were asked to characterise their research institution (number of researchers, number of PhD students, number of full-time employees providing data management support), as well as their engagement activity (target group, main drivers, activity cost, ease of implementation at a different institution) by responding to quantitative questions (see the survey template[5] for the details of questions and possible answers). For example, to estimate the

4 Iza Witkowska, 'The Survey Researcher Engagement with Data Management: What Works?' (22 July 2019), *Zenodo*, http://doi.org/10.5281/zenodo.3345305

5 Ibid.

cost of running the activity, respondents were asked to select one of five ranked options, ranging from 'inexpensive' to 'expensive'. Respondents were not asked to elaborate on their choices, or justify them.

We received 234 responses. Of these, 90 were complete and provided details describing the engagement activities, such as the activity objective, description, challenges and opportunities associated with the activity, etc. Responses that provided enough information to understand the activity were considered as valid responses and used for further selection of the most innovative activities.

The final selection of case studies was done by five volunteers. Each volunteer was asked to select 20 to 25 cases, which, based on their RDM knowledge and experience, looked innovative, inspiring and applicable to research institutions worldwide. There were no other criteria used for the selection process. To make sure that important engagement activities were not omitted from this study, the volunteers were also asked to suggest other innovative activities that they were aware of, but which were not submitted through the survey.

All cases selected by volunteers were used for the final selection. This selection was made based on the overlap between these five different lists. If a case study was listed on three or more of the five lists, it made it to the final list. In this way, 24 cases made it to this final list. Out of these, 17 were activities submitted via the survey and 7 were new activities. The list was discussed and approved, first by the five volunteers and afterwards by the entire project group.

In the next stage, we undertook hour-long interviews with 'respondents' of all shortlisted cases in order to collect missing information, quotes and photos. The interviews were recorded, transcribed and shared with the writing team.

To write the book, we organized a three-day 'book sprint' in The Hague, Netherlands. Six writers and two editors (one on-site and one working remotely), took part in the book sprint. Cases were grouped into eight themes, based on the main focus of the activity: policy, data management plans, training, events, community networks, dedicated consultants, interviews and data from senior researchers. All cases were divided between the writers, written up using the collected information, and then reviewed and edited with the help of the writers. By the end of the three days the first draft of the book was finished. After the book sprint, the editing work continued, and final versions of each case study were sent to respondents for their approval during the following week. Subsequently, the book was publicly shared for consultation, and editing continued on an ongoing basis in response to community feedback.[6]

6 Draft book with full version and comment history available online: https://docs.google.com/document/d/1XnXJeOocmaz-xU0oTmMLpBXrcFTdHmBDQG8bHMq7_GY/

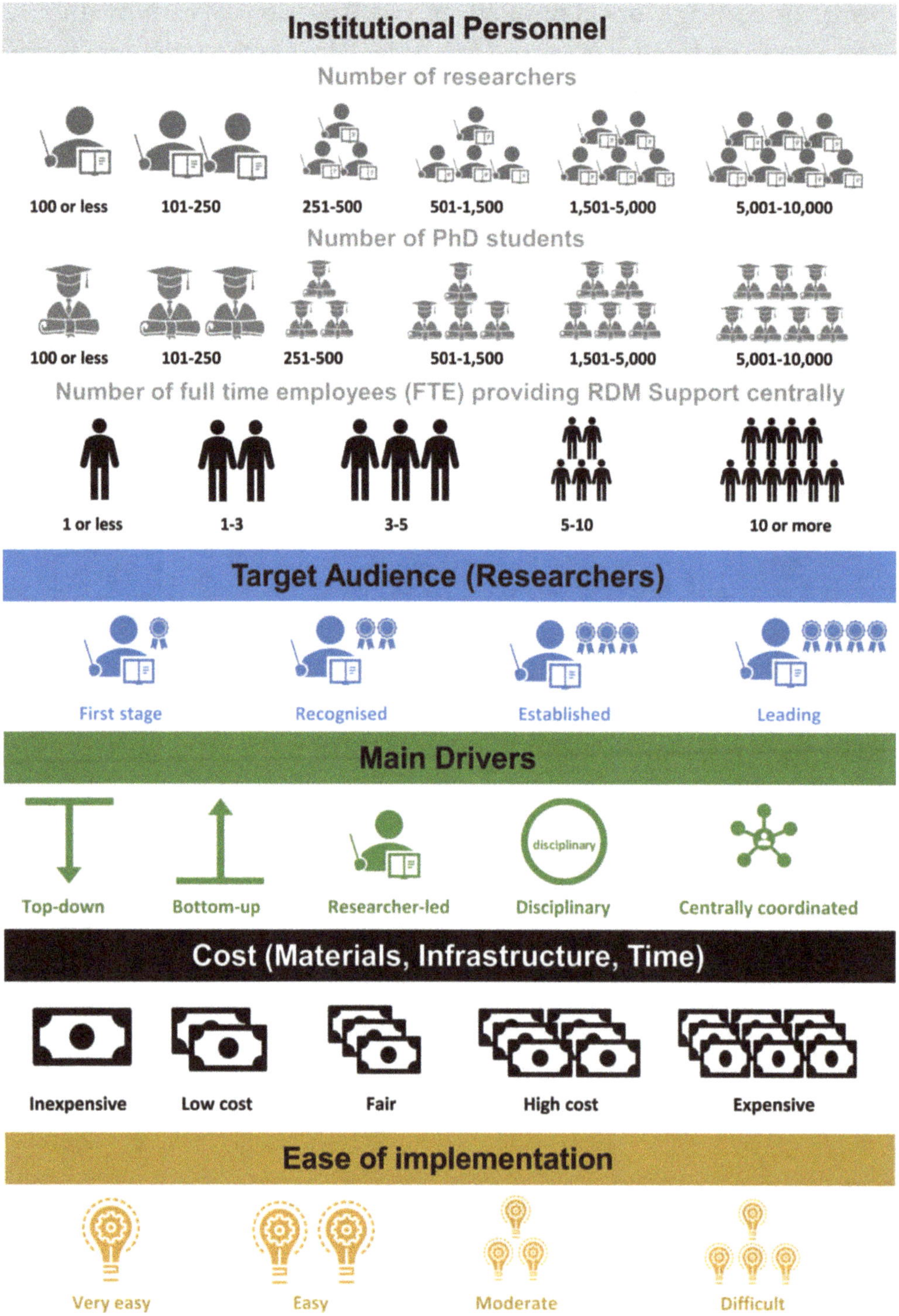


Table I. Graphical representation of the key ingredients of each case study, CC BY 4.0.

# III. How to Use this Cookbook

This infographic (Table I, left) has been designed to help you to navigate case studies of interest, and to select those most suitable for implementation within your research institution. Just like a cookbook recipe, we provide a list of 'key ingredients' in a graphical format: the elements you'll need to successfully implement each initiative.

In addition, we also provide a table (Table II, below) with a quick overview of all case studies and recipes (ingredients) necessary to implement them. You can use this quick overview to navigate directly to cases which might be most relevant to the situation at your institution (for example, the amount of resources available to you to engage with researchers).

| | 1.1 | 1.2 | 2.1 | 2.2 | 2.3 | 3.1 | 3.2 | 3.3 | 3.4 | 4.1 | 4.2 |
|---|---|---|---|---|---|---|---|---|---|---|---|
| No of researchers | | | | | | | | | | | |
| No of PhDs | | | | | | | | | | | |
| Target audience | | | | | | | | | | | |
| Main drivers | | | | | | | | | | | |
| Ease of implementation | | | | | | | | | | | |
| FTEs for RDM | | | | | | | | | | | |
| Costs materials | | | | | | | | | | | |
| Costs infrastructure | | | | | | | | | | | |
| Costs people | | | | | | | | | | | |

Table II. Overview of all cases and their key ingredients, CC BY 4.0.

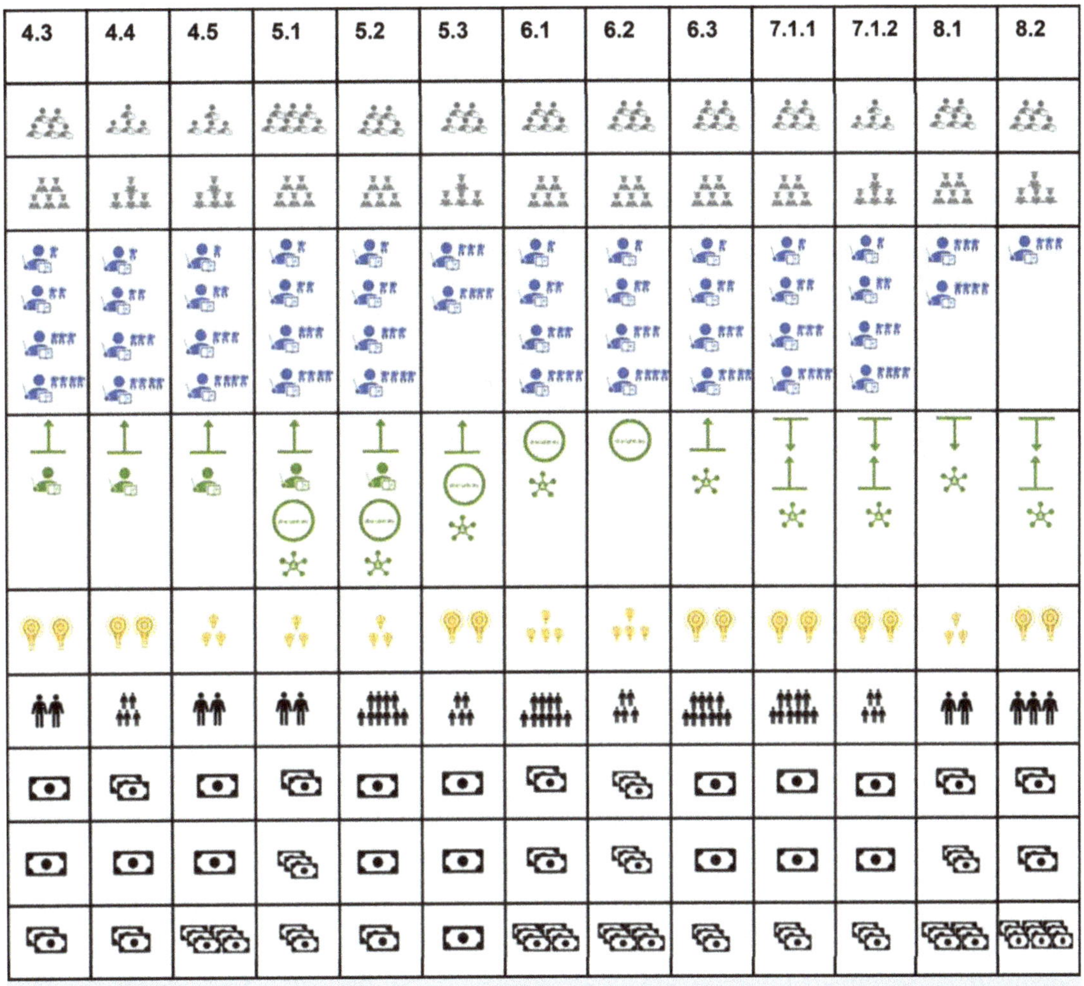


Table II. (continued from previous page).

# CASE STUDIES

data
staff
can
Data
need
Leiden
start
new
use
many
change
central
across
awareness
Centre
good
Policy
Digital
institutes
work
discuss
talk
Fieke
needs
faculties
Libraries
level
way
two
thematic
every
sharing
Services
views
engage
access
clear
Figure
One
raise
years
current
help
still
plan
believes
ensure
board
whole
network
networks
success
senior
members
session
matrix
service
easier
ideal
using
says
whilst
also
agree
tools
support
library
Schools
arose
prove
ongoing
begun
Affairs
came
learnt
will
see
case
chance
place
begin
order
may
It's
DVC
one

# 1. Research Data Management Policy: The Holy Grail of Data Management Support?

One of the easiest but most impactful ways to engage with researchers is to create awareness about the need for good Research Data Management (RDM) and then agree on what good RDM looks like. Upon this foundation many other services and activities can be built.

In this chapter, we introduce two case studies that demonstrate how engaging with researchers can create this foundation by:

1. Getting the concept of RDM accepted.
2. Collaborating to define what is meant by good RDM and to agree a policy to achieve this.
3. Following up with researchers to ensure the policy is implemented.

Both case studies are relatively inexpensive to implement if enthusiastic and talented staff are available but require access to influential people or administrative support structures.

# 1.1. Are You a Research Data Superhero? One Person Making a Big Difference at Makerere University

*Author: Joanne Yeomans*
*Contributor: Joseph Ssebulime*

*Makerere University demonstrates how one person can start engaging with researchers about data management before any formal institutional resources or services are in place.*

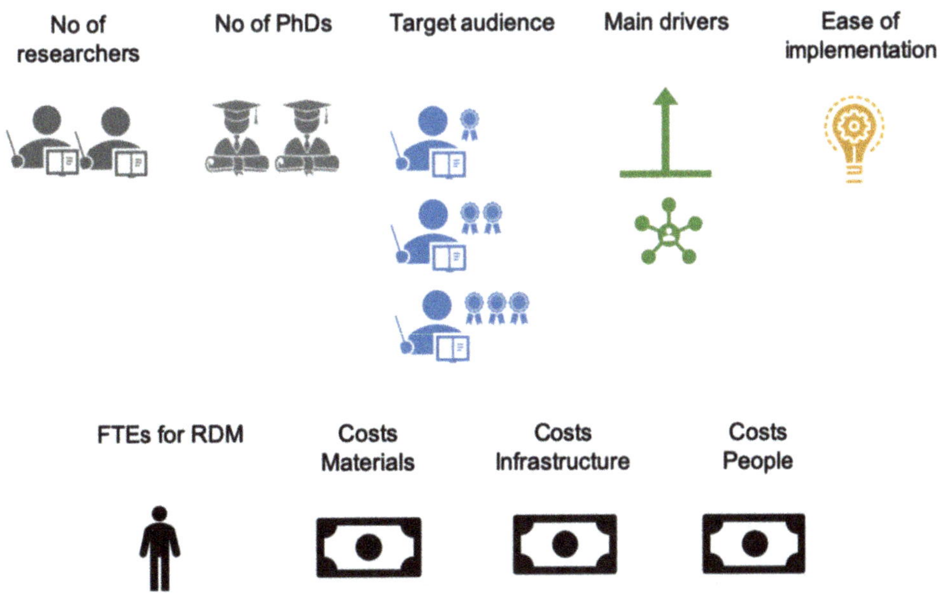


Table 1.1, CC BY 4.0.

 https://doi.org/10.11647/OBP.0185.01

In September 2017, Joseph Ssebulime interviewed research staff at Makerere University about their views on sharing their research data. Every one of them saw sharing or even storing their data anywhere but on their own computer as a loss of control over their work and an unwelcome interference, so they were far from ready to discuss the possible implementation of a university policy for research data management. Less than two years later, Joseph is thinking about speaking to them again to see if their views are still the same. What has happened in that period that might have changed their mind?

## Changing the Mindset of Researchers

After graduating in Records and Archives Management from Makerere University in 2015, Joseph was working in the university library as a Reference Librarian and searching for a topic for his Master's study. He explained how his interest came about:

> ***I came across Research Data Management (RDM) as a concept and realised that Makerere was lacking these services so I decided to research what RDM support meant, and then investigate the views of Makerere researchers about data sharing. I thought they would be interested in how their data could be looked after and re-used***

Joseph sought out individuals who had published research papers in the previous five years and recorded interviews with them. 'I was really surprised that they had no interest in changing their data management habits,' he admitted. Astonished at the lack of enthusiasm for RDM services, he was unsure what to do next.

Luckily, an opportunity arose to speak with the Deputy Vice Chancellor (DVC) for Academic Affairs and, upon proposing that Makerere University needed to implement a data management policy, Joseph found in him a strong ally. They both believed that it is essential to start with a research data management policy as a foundation.

With the support of the DVC, Makerere University is at the beginning of its RDM policy journey. Maintaining engagement with the researchers is an important priority as this will help to 'change their mindset' by addressing their concerns and then finding infrastructure solutions that work for them.

## Never Overlook an Opportunity to Speak about RDM

Joseph takes advantage of every occasion he can find to discuss the need for good RDM with researchers. He seeks opportunities at conferences and other university events to approach Makerere research staff and start a conversation about their data. His aim is to sensitize them to the need for good practice, so that the introduction of a policy and its associated procedures becomes easier. His personal enthusiasm drives him to continually look for opportunities to raise awareness about RDM whilst carrying out his job as a Reference Librarian.

Fig. 1.1.1 Conferences offer a great way to network with researchers: Joseph Ssebulime discusses data management with a conference participant at the University of Pretoria, August 2018. Photograph by Anthony Izuchukwu, CC BY 4.0.

At Makerere University there is no network drive, meaning that most researchers rely on their personal computer to store their work. A training session on 'Backing up information online using Google

Fig. 1.1.2 Poster showing a visual representation of the RDM Roadmap for Makerere University used to raise publicity and start discussions with research staff and senior university managers at meetings and conferences.[1] By Joseph Ssebulime, CC BY 4.0.

1 Poster submitted to the 2018 IFLA Library and Information Congress: Joseph Balikuddembe Ssebulime, Martie Van Deventer and Heila Pienaar, 'The role Academic Libraries could play in sensitizing researchers about research data management: a case of Makerere University Library', Session 153 — Poster Session, IFLA WLIC 2018 — 'Transform Libraries, Transform Societies', Kuala Lumpur, Malaysia, 27 August 2018, http://library.ifla.org/id/eprint/2297

Drive' provided a valuable service for researchers as well as an ideal opportunity to talk with them more generally about RDM.

Another such opportunity arose during training on how to use the institutional preprint repository. 'Open access' is a well-known and accepted concept at Makerere University so it was natural to run training sessions on uploading articles to the repository, and these sessions are well-attended. Because some publishers now also require authors to publish the data underlying their article, Joseph can include some data management topics in this training session and use it as another chance to talk about RDM.

Social media is another obvious way to reach people at the university, and Facebook posts are effective in helping to raise awareness about RDM.

## How Fast Do Things Change?

Joseph believes that the impact of his activity on driving cultural change is 'a little bit slow but very steady'. It's useful to have an 'elevator pitch' ready for when an opportunity arises, and he advises anyone interested in driving data management awareness to 'start by having conversations with as many stakeholders as possible across the university; this can begin with a brief discussion whenever there is a chance to talk to a senior official;' if they are convinced, these conversations pave the way for more formal approaches and proposals. It's clear that having a confident personality is beneficial for success, but with the right people in place Joseph believes that 'every academic institution across the country' can implement this activity. Are you the person who can do it?

## Additional Resources

Ssebuline, Joseph, Van Deventer, Martie, and Pienaar, Heila, 'The Role Academic Libraries Could Play in Developing Research Data Management Services: A Case of Makerere University Library', [Preprint], 5 July 2018, https://www.researchgate.net/publication/326208493

# 1.2. Does a Policy Solve Everything? Policy as a Driver for Engagement at Leiden University

*Author: Joanne Yeomans*

*Contributors: Fieke Schoots, Laurents Sesink*

*The Centre for Digital Scholarship at Leiden University reaches out directly to research institutes to understand the support they need to implement RDM policy.*

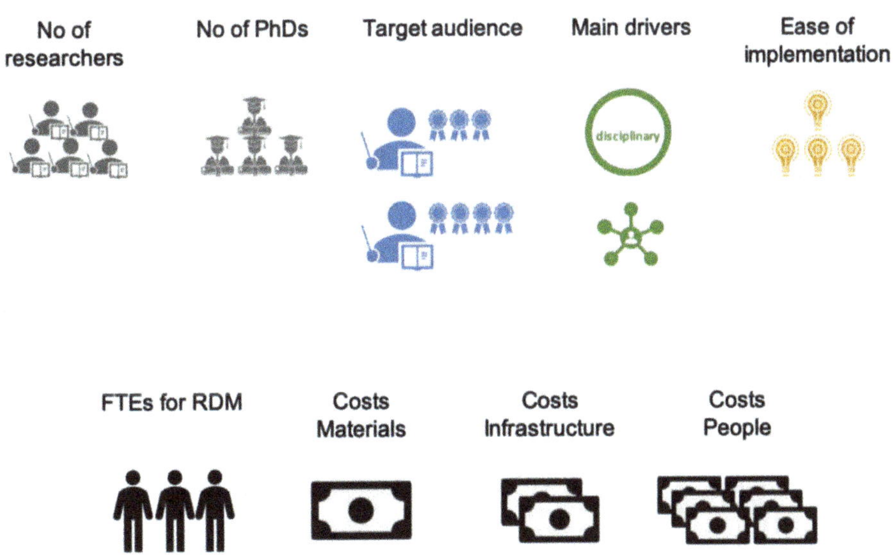


Table 1.2, CC BY 4.0.

 https://doi.org/10.11647/OBP.0185.02

## A Crown Is Merely a Hat that Lets the Rain In

A Research Data Management (RDM) policy can outline expectations but by itself will rarely engender a change of behaviour. Worse, although it may be the culmination of many months or years of work, it may prove to be 'merely a hat that lets the rain in' if not properly implemented, exposing gaps in service provision and support, and magnifying the resistance that academics feel towards administrative tasks that take them away from their research.

Engaging researchers to help produce a practical plan for implementing an RDM policy can, however, prove to be an ideal way of learning first-hand what they need to support their data management. The policy can therefore become the 'crown' that demonstrates the effectiveness and success of the resulting RDM services.

## Leiden's Use of its RDM Policy to Prompt Discussion

Leiden University Libraries' Centre for Digital Scholarship is taking the RDM discussion directly to researchers, by engaging with individual researchers on a one-to-one basis and by reaching out to research institutes and finding out what they need in order to be able to implement the Leiden University RDM Regulations[1] approved in 2016.

'We can use our RDM policy as the reason to arrange a meeting and discuss what is expected by the university in terms of data management,' says Fieke Schoots, a Data Management Expert at the Centre for Digital Scholarship who initiated and coordinates the data management activities at Leiden University Libraries. Once a meeting is underway, 'we can use the policy as a focus for finding out what is needed, by an individual or a research group, to improve their data management and so we can plan to work on solutions to make their data management easier.' These solutions help to provide incentives that result in compliance with the policy.

The result is an environment where researchers know where to go to ask for support with their data management and the central support

1 Research Data Management Regulations, Leiden University, April 2016, https://www.library.universiteitleiden.nl/binaries/content/assets/ul2ub/research--publish/research-data-management-regulations-leiden-university_def.pdf

services have a better understanding of the practical needs of the research staff regarding their research data.

## 'One Size' Does Not Fit All

The Leiden policy regulations recognise that disciplinary differences exist for many practical data management decisions and, therefore, avoid imposing a 'one-size-fits-all' solution. The regulations indicate explicitly where departments and institutes should devise their own procedures, and include a whole section on 'elaboration' that lists the specific decisions that need to be taken at a faculty or institutional level to supplement the generic policy.

Implementation of the regulations was expected to be completed by 2019 and was to be carried out jointly by the faculties and various central services: the ICT (Information, Communication and Technology) Shared Services, Academic Affairs, Information Management, and the Centre for Digital Scholarship. Some progress was made with some faculties, but by 2018 it became clear that the levels of engagement required to bring about change across the entire University were beyond the current staffing capacity. The implementation period was, therefore, extended to the end of 2020 and new support staff appointments began.

## Why Does this Kind of Engagement Take Time?

In early 2019, two members of the university library visited every faculty board to discuss the needs for support regarding open access, data management (including the procedures and services needed to elaborate and implement the policy), and the use of digital tools and methodologies. Regarding data management there were still too many diverse needs at the faculty level and so a new round of talks has begun with the 29 institutional scientific committees.[2]

To begin the conversation, a report on the current data management support for researchers in each institute has been produced, using enquiry and training statistics and a qualitative description of the

2 Leiden University Scientific Institutes, https://www.universiteitleiden.nl/en/about-us/management-and-organisation/faculties/institutes

current relevant services. This kind of engagement is staff- and time-intensive to organize and carry out.

Although the absence of dedicated staff was slowing the pace of change, it was not the only problem. 'Research staff were sometimes reluctant to start discussing new services whilst still waiting for solutions to long-standing problems,' says Fieke. It was clear that solutions would need to be delivered to persuade research staff to engage in new discussions. As a result, several pilot projects have begun in parallel to develop solutions for the storage of legacy data sets and encryption tools.

## Continuing the Engagement with a Matrix of Support Services

In order to improve the connections between staff, maintain the ongoing engagement, and deliver solutions, the steering board has agreed to a new approach to organising and strengthening support that employs both decentralised and centralised expertise (see Fig. 1.2.1).

Fieke explained this new approach:

> ***The matrix identifies key support themes, such as ethics and legal advice, where there are existing staff both in central support units and embedded within the faculties or institutes. Upon this matrix you can build multidisciplinary and thematic networks to bring these staff members together at a faculty level and a theme level, respectively.***

The first thematic 'Data Management Network' event was organised by the Centre for Digital Scholarship in June 2019. It brought together embedded data stewards, central RDM support staff, and researchers who are particularly active in data management from across the whole university, to talk about their priorities for developments to improve data management practice.

Through this meeting, central support staff have already learnt more about the research processes and needs of researchers, and researchers have learnt more about the expertise and possibilities offered by further engagement with central support staff.

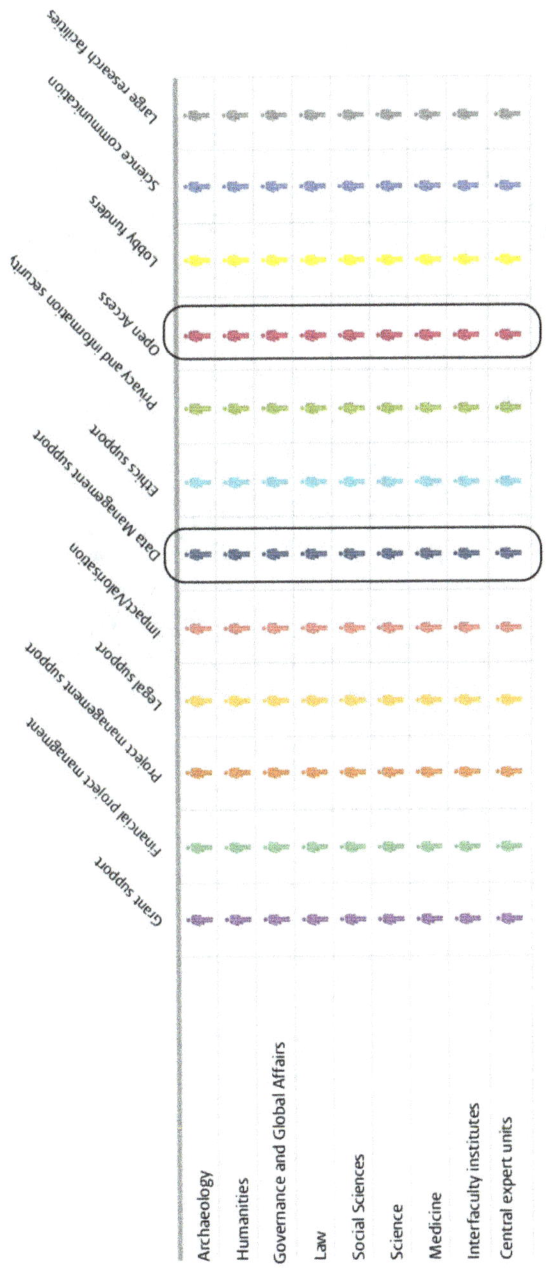


Fig. 1.2.1 Leiden University's proposed thematic and disciplinary networks, 2019. By Marcel Villerius, Leiden University, CC BY 4.0.

The ongoing efforts to engage researchers have been very rewarding for both sides, but have also been necessary to ensure that the regulations are a welcome tool for change.

Fig. 1.2.2 Leiden University's Data Management Network convening event, 27 June 2019. Leiden University Libraries, CC BY 4.0.

data
can
Data
will
staff
team
time
plan
also
process
Unit
right
work
engage
help
might
form
policy
department
projects
library
start
need
clear
it's
able
service
still
stub
next
write
case

# 2. Finding Triggers for Engagement

Despite the benefits of data management planning for the researcher, many still regard it as an administrative burden. Interestingly, some institutions were able to turn data management planning into an opportunity to engage researchers in discussions about data.

This chapter looks at several case studies where workflows have been designed to bring about interaction and engagement at key moments in the research process.

Being able to work in collaboration with other support or management units within the university was a key factor in each of these.

# 2.1. Taking Advantage of Existing Administrative Systems: MRC/CSO Social and Public Health Sciences Unit, University of Glasgow

*Authors: Joanne Yeomans, Iza Witkowska*

*Contributor: Mary-Kate Hannah*

*Piggybacking onto an existing system for approving research proposals, the Health Sciences Unit at the University of Glasgow automatically contacts researchers that might need RDM support at the beginning of their projects, and then follows up throughout the project's lifespan.*

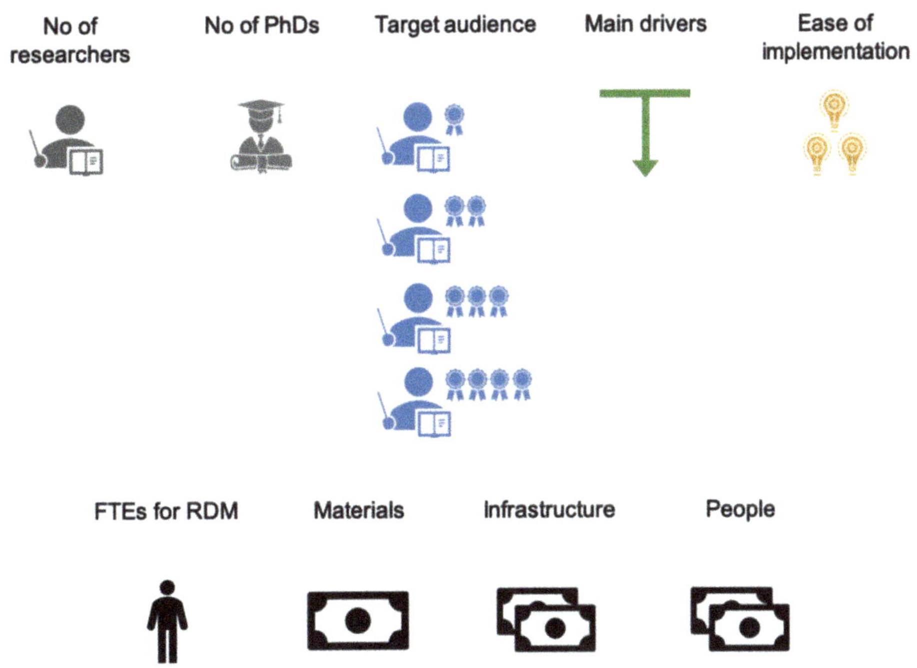


Table 2.1, CC BY 4.0.

 https://doi.org/10.11647/OBP.0185.03

## Engagement as Early as Possible — The WHY

In the MRC/CSO Social and Public Health Sciences Unit at the University of Glasgow,[1] the department representatives decided to use an existing administrative reporting system to help engage with researchers about data management issues and to manage requests coming to the IT (Information Technology) and other support staff offices.

> ***Part of the reason we set up this system is that people would apply for grants, and then when the research started they'd go to the support staff and ask: can you help me with transcribing, can you help me with fieldwork or whatever else was needed, and the support staff representative would say: we don't have this in our diary, we have two other surveys happening at the moment, so we can't do this, we need warning that these things are going to happen. So now, because it's reported in advance in the system, they can plan, they can take on new staff, anything that is needed. — Mary-Kate Hannah, Data Scientist in the Unit.***

## How Early Is Early? The HOW

Whenever a project is initiated, a researcher has to fill in and submit an online form. The research proposal is considered by the 'Portfolio Group' which checks that the topic is in line with the unit's focus and identifies what resources might be needed within the department, whether space for staff members, IT facilities, and so on.

The Portfolio Group consists of senior and experienced research staff, and senior representatives of all the different research programmes. Representatives from various support offices also sit in on the meetings. The group considers the proposal and, among other things, identifies whether there is data collection or data creation planned and whether data will be stored at Glasgow University. If so, they tick a box in the form that indicates a data management plan (DMP) is required and

1 MRC/CSO Social and Public Health Sciences Unit at the University of Glasgow receives joint core funding from the Medical Research Council (MRC) and the Scottish Government Chief Scientist Office (CSO).

this triggers an automatic email to Mary-Kate and to the submitter so that they can follow this up. Without Mary-Kate signing off on the completion of a satisfactory DMP, the researcher cannot move forward with their grant application or their research.

The automated email starts the process of putting Mary-Kate in touch with the researcher to assist with the writing of the plan. This happens regardless of whether a funder requires a DMP or not: if the research is going to generate data that will be stored at Glasgow University, then the department itself still requires a DMP to get things right from the start.

Fig. 2.1.1 Mary-Kate Hannah helping a researcher to complete a DMP at the MRC/CSO Social and Public Health Sciences Unit, University of Glasgow. Photograph by Enni Pulkkinen, 2019, CC BY 4.0.

## Benefits for the Researcher — The WHAT

So, what happens after the sending of the automated email saying that a DMP is needed? The next step involves Mary-Kate sending a customized email and flagging up resources such as the pre-filled DMP template and the DMPonline tool, as well as offering support on any other Research Data Management (RDM) relevant aspect (for example, handling personal data). She also refers researchers to a recorded presentation about RDM consisting of PowerPoint slides with recorded voiceover. This personal touch is definitely the key factor in making the implementation of this process successful.

The RDM support doesn't end there. Once a project begins, a study or trial master file[2] is set up on the network drive and customized for the project team. It has standard folders for storing common administrative documentation, such as grant application and legal documents, and includes a folder for data management. This generic folder structure was developed after looking at and reviewing many studies at the department. 'Researchers and support staff are very happy with this; it saves time as they don't have to think about this themselves,' says Mary-Kate.

Fig. 2.1.2 Mary-Kate Hannah delivering a training session on data management planning at the MRC/CSO Social and Public Health Sciences Unit, University of Glasgow. Photograph by Enni Pulkkinen, 2019, CC BY 4.0.

2 Trial master file, https://en.wikipedia.org/wiki/Trial_master_file

## Looking Back, Does It Work?

Yes, it does! People are getting used to the idea of planning their data management: because they did it for their last project, they are expecting it for their next project. They have often reported that the process of writing the DMP has been helpful and that they have found conversations with the research data management advisor to be useful.

Having said that, there is still room for improvement in the system to save researchers' time. For example, researchers need to write similar details in different forms for their grant application, their ethical review request, and their DMP. These forms are delivered at different times and the procedural timing could be better optimized.

Sometimes the detailed information requested in the DMP comes too late, for example, 'the researcher might have had ethical approval for their data collection consent form which did not contain data-sharing information, then they start to write their data management plan and realize that they will have to make an amendment to their consent form and ask for an amendment to their ethics application,' says Mary-Kate.

What is clear though, is that embedding a requirement for data management planning directly in the unit's authorization process is crucial in getting researchers to think about their data management at an early stage, and in putting RDM support staff in contact with researchers right from the start.

# 2.2. Engaging with Researchers through Data Management Planning at the University of Manchester

*Author: Joanne Yeomans*

*Contributors: Rosie Higman, Christopher Gibson*

***The University of Manchester illustrates how careful design of DMP templates and DMP policies allows staff to effectively engage with researchers through DMP review.***

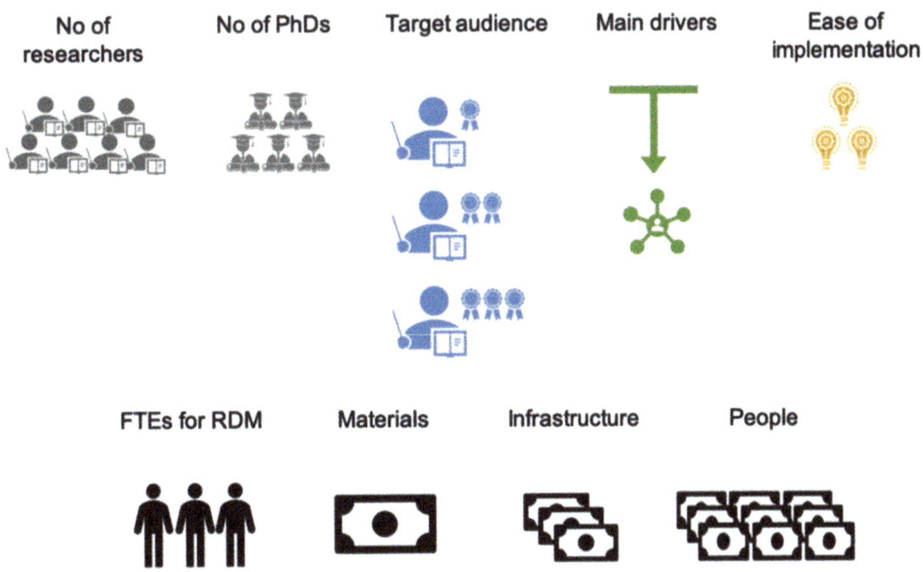


Table 2.2, CC BY 4.0.

 https://doi.org/10.11647/OBP.0185.04

Requiring an approved Data Management Plan (DMP) before allowing a research project to begin might work for smaller units within a university, but it might not scale up across a large research-intensive university. The University of Manchester has found a way to design their DMP template and DMP requirement process so that the library support team can potentially engage with all researchers at an early stage of their research. Focusing the engagement around the writing of the DMP means that they can offer advice when a researcher is beginning their project, but they can also learn first-hand whether the university's data management policies are practical.

At the University of Manchester, a DMP is required when applying for funding, ethics approval and/or IT storage. 'Between these you encompass most research at the university,' thinks Rosie Higman, Research Services Librarian. 'I'm not saying we've got it perfect but at least in theory, we're going to cover most projects through these routes.'

The University has DMP templates in the DMPonline[3] system that ask university-specific questions in the first section (see Fig. 2.2.1). These include questions about storage needs and whether the research is handling personal data using a tick-box format so that the questions are easier to answer. The University's Information Governance Office uses this part of the form as the asset register in accordance with the European General Data Protection Regulation (GDPR).

The Research Data Management team (Fig. 2.2.2) in Research Services at the university library check this first section of every DMP and give feedback to the submitter.

3 DMPonline tool, https://dmponline.dcc.ac.uk

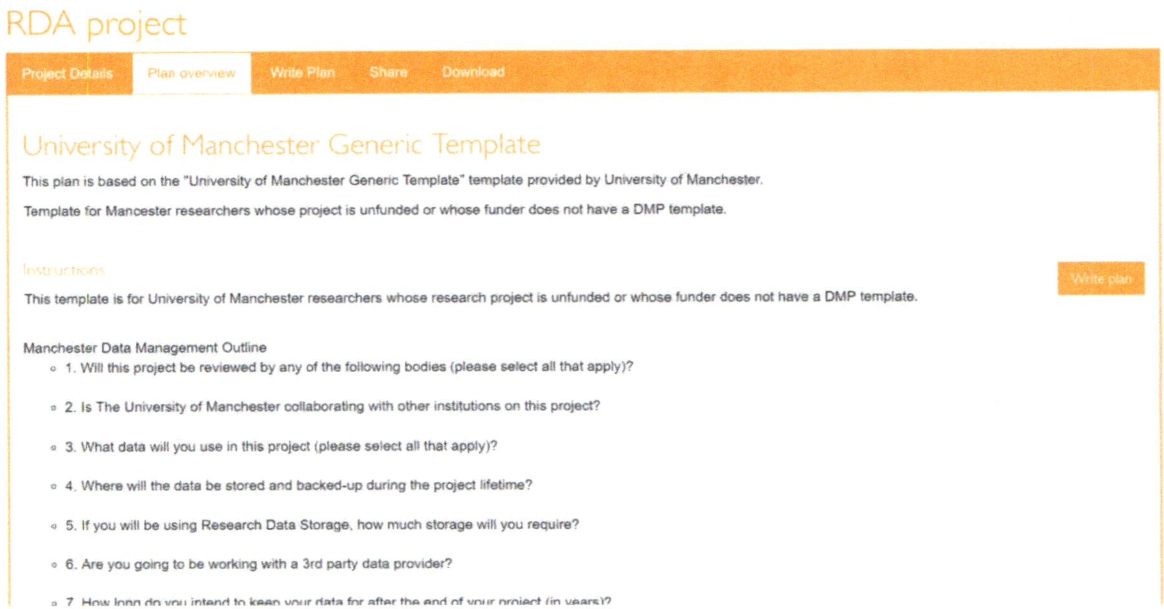


Fig. 2.2.1 Overview of the University of Manchester DMPonline template showing the Manchester-specific questions. University of Manchester Library, CC BY 4.0.

Fig 2.2.2 University of Manchester Research Data Management team. From left to right: Jess Napthine-Hodgkinson (Research Services Officer); Clare Liggins (Research Services Librarian); Chris Gibson (Research Services Librarian). Rosie Higman has since started a new position at the University of Sheffield. University of Manchester Library, CC BY 4.0.

## What Do You Learn from Checking So Many DMPs?

'You can certainly tell which DMPs are from people who have been to our training,' Rosie is pleased to point out. 'It's helped us work out where we have lots of gaps, where the policy is unrealistic or the procedures are unsupportable.' She gives an example: 'There's a university procedure for when a researcher makes a recording of a participant; it's clear and well written and has been around for some time, but it suggests that every researcher should have access to an encrypted recording device and the university is only just working out what the cost of that would be.'

When talking to researchers about a DMP, you are therefore sometimes challenged, 'how do you do that in practice?' In the case of encrypted recordings, the Research Data Management (RDM) team, with the help of information governance and IT (Information Technology), has been able to draw up a list of practical steps a researcher can take, but this has raised difficult questions about whether the policy should stand. 'It's making our services more responsive to what researchers want,' concludes Rosie.

## Avoiding Being a Victim of Your Own Success

Almost 20% of the submitters request a more detailed review of their DMP and most of these requests are from researchers dealing with personal data or ethical permissions.

Rosie and her team have some standardised answers, which an officer tailors to each case before drafting a response. One of three librarians will then review the officer's comments and enhance them with more discipline-specific suggestions. They aim to treat each plan in under an hour. 'We already spend significant time on this and every week meet to discuss the DMP review requests that have come in and how we can balance them with our other work priorities. If the demand increases, we're not yet sure how to address this,' admits Rosie.

One technique that they believe will save review time is to remove the option to allow free text and instead offer tick-boxes in answer to fixed questions. The use of pre-drafted comments for responses has also helped, but the time it takes to review a single DMP is still a challenge.

The use of DMPonline started in Manchester in 2018, when the European GDPR also came into effect. Although all researchers are required by university policy[4] to write a DMP, it's not clear what proportion of researchers are doing so. The university also has a system for tracking student progress in general, which requires students to have a conversation with their supervisor, during which there is a prompt to check that the student has a DMP. 'This is a good start, but obviously carries the risk that if a supervisor does not care about data management then students will not create a DMP,' says Rosie.

With just over a year of experience in using DMPonline in this way, the library team thinks it is a good time to review the level of compliance. They will do this by checking the institutional records to identify the proportion of research projects that have a DMP and expressing this as a percentage for the university, faculties and schools. The results, expected in late 2019, will be interesting to compare differences in behaviour and should give the team some idea of how demand for reviews might increase.

4 University of Manchester Research Data Management Policy, http://documents.manchester.ac.uk/DocuInfo.aspx?DocID=33802

# 2.3. Timing Is Everything When It Comes to Engaging with Researchers at the University of Technology Sydney

*Author: Iza Witkowska*

*Contributors: Wendy Liu, Duncan Loxton, Elizabeth Stokes, Sharyn Wise*

***At the University of Sydney, support staff provide grant recipients with 'stub' DMPs and interviews at the right time to maximize researcher engagement.***

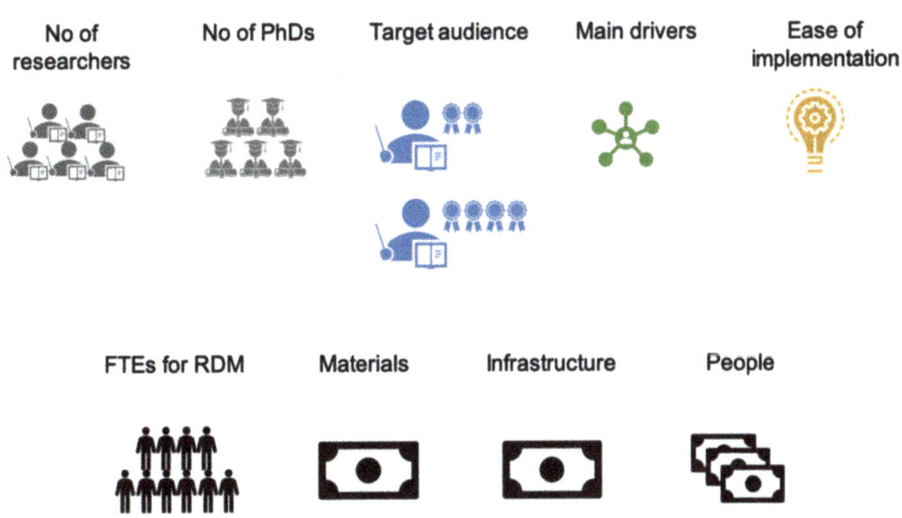


Table 2.3, CC BY 4.0.

 https://doi.org/10.11647/OBP.0185.05

At the University of Technology Sydney, the eResearch Unit[5] in the Central IT (Information Technology) Division and the Library's Research Data Team[6] collaboratively approach recipients of major research grants and offer them a 45-minute interview to provide data management support and create a data management plan (DMP). The aim of this activity is to help grant recipients to comply with the data management plan policy from Australia's major research funders and to simultaneously engage them with discussions about research data.

Many Research Data Management (RDM) support services within universities and research institutions do this, so what makes the work by the team from the University of Technology Sydney so successful and noteworthy? Well, it's all in the details.

First, they come to researchers with a 'stub' DMP: a pre-filled DMP based on the abstract of the funded grant application. This advance work helps to make things run more smoothly and means they can structure the interview around whether the draft plan accurately characterises the researchers' data management activities and requirements. And why does this approach work? Well, as the saying goes 'you catch more flies with honey than with vinegar'. The stub DMP is the 'honey' because it takes researchers one step closer to meeting funders' requirements. The expected outcome of the interview is not to have a completed DMP, but to have started a conversation about data management.

Second, persistence. It's not always easy to get the lead investigator to respond to the first contact, but our colleagues from Sydney don't give up. They repeatedly attempt to schedule an interview, and will approach more junior researchers on the project, especially those responsible for data curation/custodianship, if the lead investigator remains unavailable.

Third, their timing is right. These interviews target research teams at the right point in the project cycle to make data management decisions. They also provide an immediate connection to eResearch support if complex software or computational infrastructure is required.

5 eResearch Unit, https://eresearch.uts.edu.au/

6 Library's Research Data Team, https://www.lib.uts.edu.au/research/research-data-management

There are benefits on both sides. Researchers engage with research data, and gain awareness of RDM infrastructure and the support available at the university before they need it. The provision of appropriate data storage solutions, software or other infrastructure for their research projects is guaranteed. Policy compliance becomes less of a hurdle, and the increase in collaboration between service units within the university helps to break down institutional silos. Librarians can demystify research data management practices for researchers in a friendly way, while gaining a deeper understanding of specific data management requirements.

The good news is that any organisation able to provide a DMP tool (in this case, Stash,[7] a home-grown service integrated into the research management system) and build communication between IT infrastructure and Library/RDM services, can implement a similar initiative. Good communication channels and the ability to provide a swift follow-up are also essential. In order to achieve this, it's helpful to have a coordinator in place, especially someone familiar with the available IT infrastructure.

To take this service to the next level, this activity can be linked to broader institutional campaigns surrounding academic integrity, raising its profile within the university. Other options are to strengthen collaboration with other research support offices and collect evidence that DMPs improve data management practices, for example, by conducting user satisfaction surveys. To secure the project in the longer term, it is also important to document and communicate its success to senior administration.

7 Stash, research data management tool, https://www.lib.uts.edu.au/research/research-data-management/research-data-management-plan-rdmp

# 3. Engagement through Training

Direct training requires substantial time and effort, but is one of the most effective ways to make people aware of the importance of Research Data Management (RDM) best practices. The following case studies are each aimed to engage researchers with research data through different training methods:

- Bring Your Own Data (B.Y.O.D.) workshop at the University of Cambridge;
- Methods Class Outreach at the University of Minnesota;
- PhD course at UiT The Arctic University of Norway;
- Open courses at UiT The Arctic University of Norway.

These cases were initiated either by individuals or a small group of RDM support staff, illustrating the potential for a few people to make a difference. The size of the relevant institutions ranges from small to large, showing how such approaches can be implemented across a diverse range of institutional settings.

## Where There's a Will, There's a Way

Don't worry if you're short of resources: our contributors had the same concerns. These activities don't cost much in terms of training materials and infrastructure, and you can select the most suitable training approaches according to the number of staff at your disposal. If you already have an RDM team in place, you can gain inspiration from UiT in Norway and focus on organising a course tailored to a particular target group. If you have concerns about the capacity of your team, you might find the cases from Cambridge and Minnesota particularly appealing. We hope that you will be inspired by these stories and that you can find suitable training methods for your own institution.

# 3.1. Bring Your Own Data (B.Y.O.D.) Workshop at the University of Cambridge

*Author: Connie Clare*

*Contributor: Annemarie Hildegard Eckes-Shephard*

*A University of Cambridge Data Champion shows how one volunteer can engage with peers and provide valuable support through leading an interactive workshop on RDM best practices.*

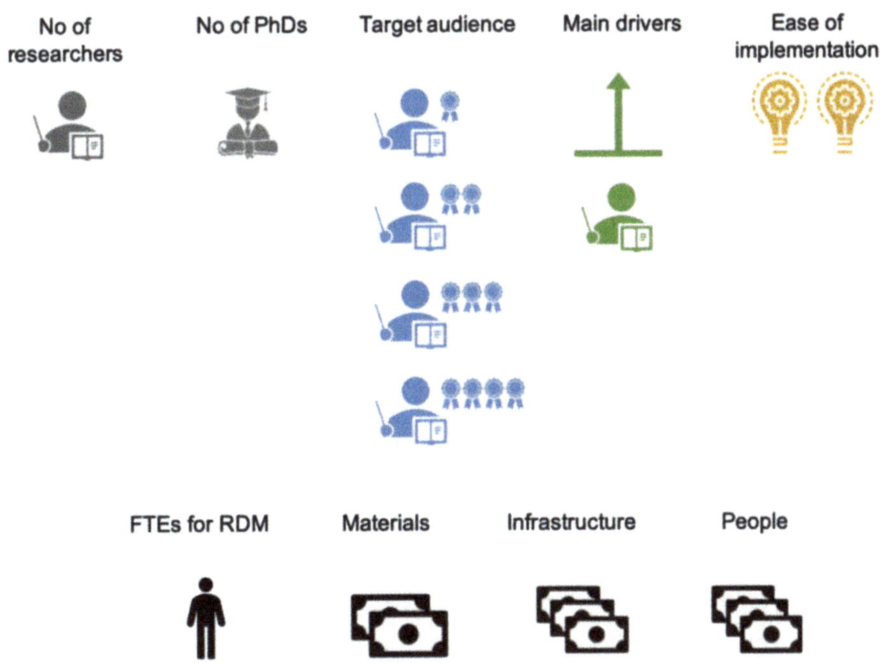


Table 3.1, CC BY 4.0.[1]

1 Note that the figures above are for the Department of Geography, University of Cambridge, and not for the University of Cambridge overall.

 https://doi.org/10.11647/OBP.0185.06

Scientific papers tend to be written and presented with clarity and structure, but most would agree that clarity and structure are not always features of the underlying raw data. Although most researchers embark on their academic journey with the intention of adhering to good data management practices, as soon as they are faced with balancing data management against the other pressing demands of a deadline-driven research schedule, it drops in priority. It rarely takes long before finding and organising files becomes a dreaded digital chore.

## A Helping Hand

University of Cambridge Data Champion, Annemarie Hildegard Eckes-Shephard, is currently undertaking a PhD in Biogeography. Her doctoral research focuses on developing a mechanistic growth model to determine how trees respond to climate change, and this research experience — together with her previous role as a crop database curator — has made Annemarie familiar with large datasets and well-equipped with tips and tricks to help others.

Annemarie understands the many challenges of managing research data and identifies time as a major constraint: 'Researchers are often too busy to allocate time for organising their digital files, yet if they could only prioritise this task, it promises to save time and frustration in the long-term.' Annemarie highlights other barriers to proper data management as 'a general lack of motivation to structure data or insufficient training on the topic': researchers simply don't know *how* or *where* to start organising their data.

## A 'B.Y.O.D.' Invitation

As an empathetic PhD student, Annemarie wanted to share her knowledge about best practice with her colleagues within the Department of Geography. She therefore started 'Bring Your Own Data' (B.Y.O.D.), a project part-funded by Jisc,[1] which brought researchers together for monthly workshops on how to organise their data to improve the quality of their research. Each two-hour workshop began with a short

1 Jisc, https://www.jisc.ac.uk/

introductory talk delivered by Annemarie to teach important aspects of data management, including:

- file-naming conventions;
- writing 'README' files (messages to future self);
- structuring files and folders;
- using a data audit framework[2] to help researchers think about their data management.

As the name implies, B.Y.O.D. encouraged participants to bring their own laptops and start organising their data in an interactive and inclusive environment. Annemarie hoped that working in a group would facilitate collaboration and networking whilst inspiring individuals to work towards open science using good data management practices. She also believed that 'making an official event in their calendar and therefore setting time aside would help researchers overcome the perception of not having enough time for data management.'

Fig. 3.1 The 'Bring Your Own Data' workshop is underway at the University of Cambridge. © Annemarie Eckes-Shephard, CC BY 4.0.

2 Data Audit Framework methodology, 26 May 2009, https://www.data-audit.eu/DAF_Methodology.pdf

## Feedback for Future Learning

Participants were asked to complete a short survey before and after each workshop to provide information about their aims and objectives for the session and how they were planning to achieve them, and to provide feedback with suggestions for how future workshops could be improved.

While B.Y.O.D. was well-received by all the participants, Annemarie admits that over time it became difficult to encourage people to attend the event, and that more support would have been required to publicise future workshops. Perhaps the use of promotional materials (for example, posters and flyers) would have increased visibility to a wider audience. Nevertheless, B.Y.O.D. is a shining example of how an individual effort can generate a demonstrable impact and drive cultural change within a research community.

# 3.2. Introducing Data Management into Existing Courses at the University of Minnesota

*Author: Yan Wang*

*Contributor: Alicia Hofelich Mohr, Jenny McBurney*

***To provide more discipline-relevant support, the University of Minnesota RDM team contacts staff who are teaching graduate research methods, and works with them to embed suitable RDM training in their courses.***

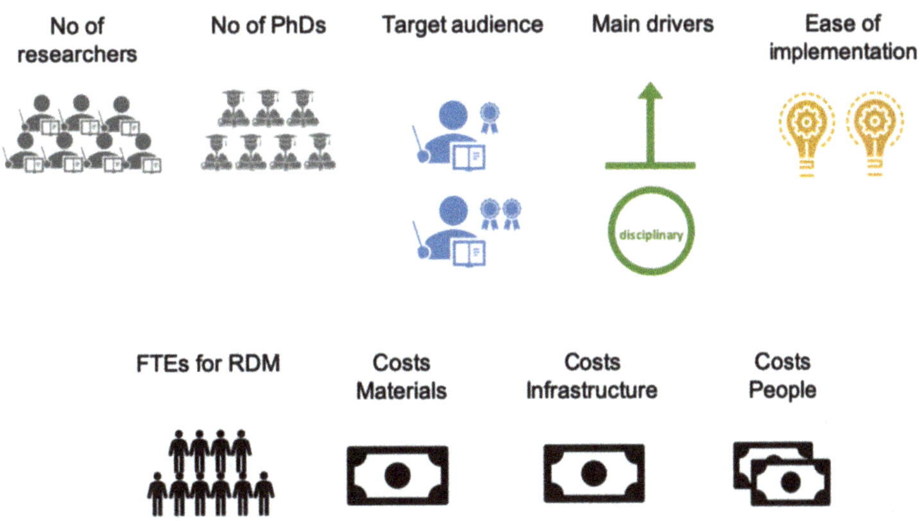


Table 3.2, CC BY 4.0.

 https://doi.org/10.11647/OBP.0185.07

## From Grassroots to Widespread Influence

Back in 2015, two recent PhD graduates working at the University of Minnesota (UMN) contacted every instructor of graduate research methods in social science, and proposed integrating disciplinary Research Data Management (RDM) education into their courses. It was a bold proposal, but since then this disciplinary RDM training has grown from its small-scale, grassroots beginnings, becoming integrated into 60 courses across 7 colleges.

Alicia Hofelich Mohr, one of these two PhD graduates, is currently a library collaborator at the College of Liberal Arts. These collaborators are disciplinary experts based at their domain-specific college, and their job is to work closely with the RDM colleagues from the library to jointly provide general and domain-specific research support, including training, to all faculty members.

The University of Minnesota has a strong culture of good RDM. This is partly thanks to its early adoption of RDM support; since 2010, the RDM team has grown from around 10 staff members to more than 25, and includes librarians and collaborators from different colleges.

Being embedded in regular research methods courses, the RDM training usually lasts between 60 to 90 minutes with a class size of five to 20 students. All courses start with the same basic RDM principles: file-naming and file organisation; data sharing; archiving; and security issues. Additional subjects are introduced depending on the discipline.

## A Lightweight Approach Makes for an Excellent Return on Investment

If you want to introduce elements of RDM training to existing courses within your institution, Alicia suggests you can 'find a few motivated people and that is really all you need to start. When you are a small team, you can do things quickly'. Their lightweight approach does not cost much but makes an excellent return on investment, and the disciplinary elements of the training clearly demonstrate the relevance of RDM to the attendees.

The training received good anecdotal feedback, and was a welcome addition to courses. Many people are now aware of RDM in general, and interest in data management has grown. The RDM training providers no longer need to approach course instructors: instead the course instructors (re)invite them, and many instructors have even found it useful to use RDM practice in their own work. The RDM training is also starting to attract the interest of researchers and principal investigators who hear about it from their students. 'Sometimes principal investigators learn about RDM through word-of-mouth, and then ask for help from us so they can incorporate the things we talk about in class into their own projects,' says Jenny McBurney, a research services librarian at the UMN Libraries.

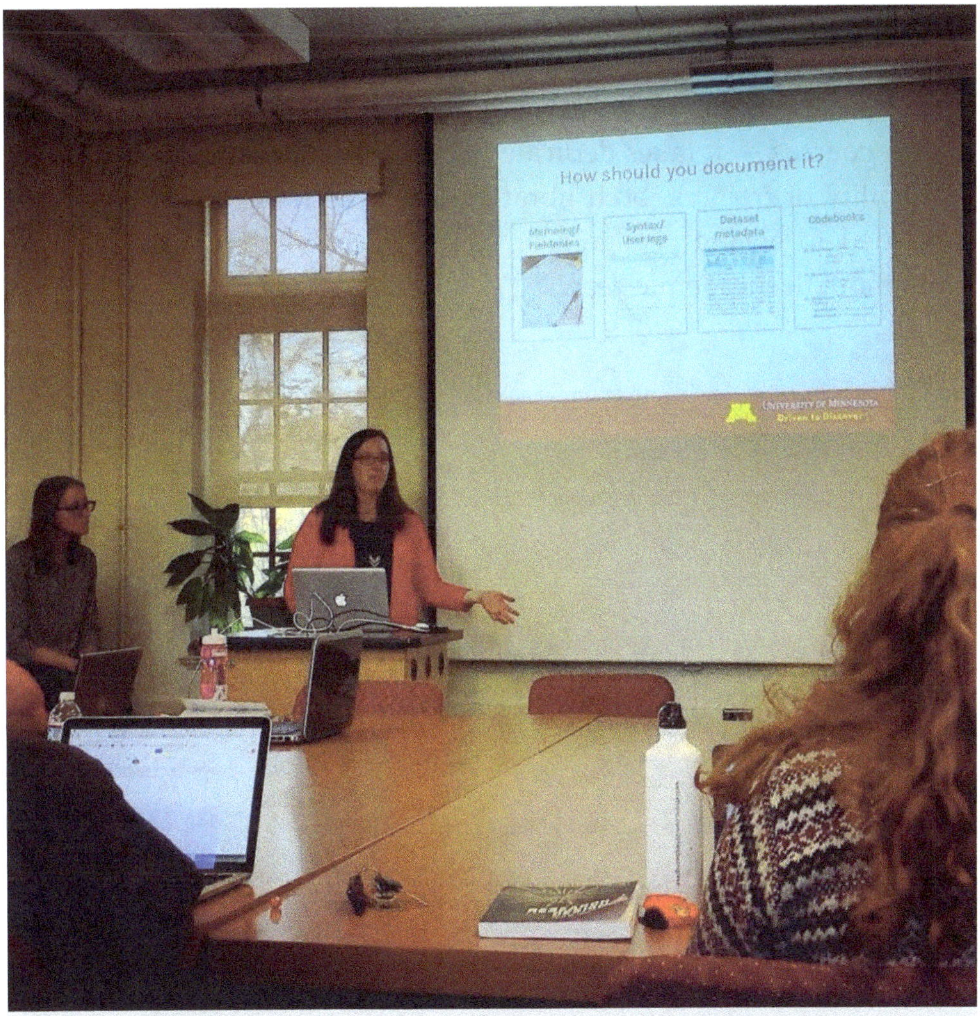


Fig. 3.2 RDM training in one of the research methods classes at the University of Minnesota. © Kate Peterson / UMN Libraries, CC BY 4.0.

## Create a Community to Make It Sustainable

'One challenge we are still facing is how to talk about RDM in disciplines where RDM is not a "thing" yet,' says Alicia. This is where you need the disciplinary collaborators: they can find the place to introduce RDM topics that resonate well with the researchers. This ensures the training delivers not just appropriate knowledge about RDM, but also engages the interest of the researchers with data management skills and provides examples of how to turn their knowledge into practice.

To keep the RDM training growing, you also need a good team. Despite the low overall cost, some time and effort are required to choose an appropriate target course, and to prepare and coordinate the delivery of topics relevant to that particular discipline. 'After a while you receive recurring course invitations; meanwhile you want to reach out to new courses — it takes dedicated people,' explains Jenny. Sufficient availability of trainers, both librarians and disciplinary collaborators, is needed to ensure coverage of courses across multiple disciplines throughout the academic year.

# 3.3. Engaging with RDM through a PhD Course on Academic Integrity and Open Science at UiT The Arctic University of Norway

*Author: Yan Wang*

*Contributor: Helene N. Andreassen*

***UiT The Arctic University of Norway engages with PhD students by embedding modular RDM training in its academic skills course, and ensuring close alignment with its other transferable skills training.***

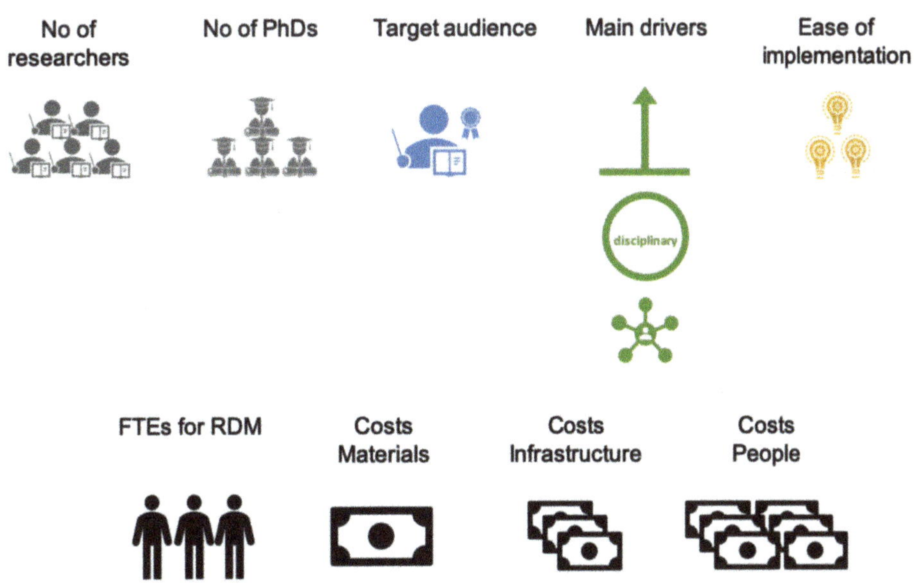


Table 3.3, CC BY 4.0.

 https://doi.org/10.11647/OBP.0185.08

## Why PhDs?

'PhDs are in most cases very positive about new developments and we should motivate them to do what is expected or required,' explains Helene N. Andreassen, the Head of Library Teaching and Learning Support at UiT The Arctic University of Norway. One of the courses Helene and her team provide is a bi-annual multidisciplinary seminar series[3] with a focus on academic integrity and open science, available to all PhD students at the institution. Since it began in 2015, participants have come from a rich variety of disciplines, and since 2019 the seminar series has been made obligatory for law students. What's more, an increasing number of participants choose Research Data Management (RDM) topics for their final essay, which is required to complete the course.

## What Works? Good Content and a Thoughtful Course Layout

In order to prepare the content of the course, the team works closely with other groups at the university, such as the research administration and the IT department. While the overall approach and the reading list are multidisciplinary, the course design still takes disciplinary differences into account by including activities that allow reflection on similarities and differences across disciplines and methodological approaches. In the RDM session participants can choose between different modules based on the type of data they deal with in their research.

After a general introduction, the course is split into groups focusing separately on data with sensitive information and data with non-sensitive information. There might not always be a perfect format that suits everyone given the heterogeneous nature of research and the increasing number of interdisciplinary studies. Nevertheless, Helene and her team continuously work on improving the content and how they deliver the course.

3 Information about the bi-annual multidisciplinary seminar series is available at https://uit.no/ub/laringsstotte#linje2

Fig. 3.3 A moment during the PhD course. © Erik Lieungh/UiT The Arctic University of Norway, CC BY-ND.

## Course Preparation is an Educational Process Itself

Ten people teach and develop the content of the whole course, with three dedicated to the RDM modules. These teachers coordinate with staff responsible for PhD programs at the faculties that give credits to students, as well as the High North Academy,[4] a special unit that coordinates all doctoral courses on transferable skills at UiT. Teachers also devote time to promoting the course through formal and informal information channels, and evaluating the exam essays.

The course preparation is, in itself, a team-building and professional development activity. The teaching group meets every month to read relevant papers and reflect upon how to support PhDs. Development of the reading list for the course is a joint task.

Contributing to the development and execution of the course is a lot of work and requires people's time and commitment. 'It is all voluntary, but very good for the team spirit, and I think we will continue doing it,' says Helene.

4 High North Academy, https://site.uit.no/hna/

## RDM Training as an Institutional Effort

RDM is an emerging subject requiring joint efforts across the university to help develop and promote it. In addition to working on their own course, the team is also in close contact with leaders of related courses, to share materials and ensure consistency of message across the curriculum. For instance, supervisors attending a course on supervising PhD students are now encouraged to send their students to complete the RDM training. The team also talks about RDM training to the university's vice-chancellor of research, whose support contributes in raising awareness across the various departments of the institution.

# 3.4. Open Courses at UiT The Arctic University of Norway

*Author: Yan Wang*

*Contributor: Helene N. Andreassen*

*Lessons learned while engaging researchers through a series of open, online RDM training courses at UiT The Arctic University of Norway.*

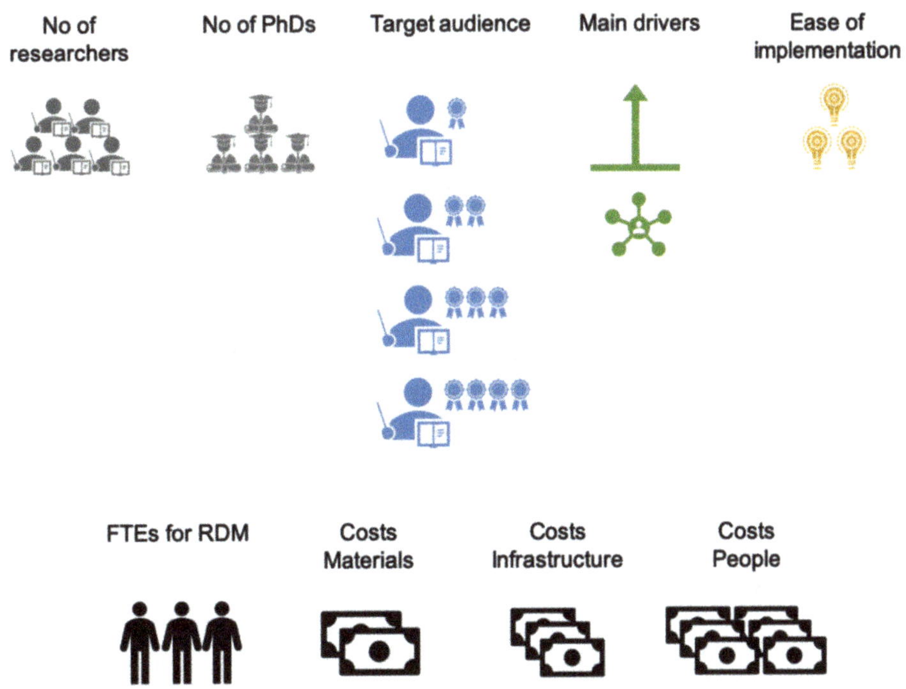


Table 3.4, CC BY 4.0.

 https://doi.org/10.11647/OBP.0185.09

## Opening the Door to RDM Training

In 2016, the library of UiT The Arctic University of Norway launched a brand new archive for open research data: UiT Open Research Data. To train researchers and graduate students how to use it, the library developed introductory courses, with time for questions and discussions. After one semester, they realised that they also needed to include more narrowly defined courses in the programme, and this opened the door to introducing various Research Data Management (RDM) topics. 'If you open one door, there will be people knocking on other doors too. For instance, when we talk about open data, there is always someone in the audience wanting to talk about sensitive data,' reflects Helene N. Andreassen, Head of Library Teaching and Learning Support.

The UiT Library has gradually developed a series of short open courses:[5] currently it consists of one introductory course focusing on the 'whys' and 'hows' of RDM, and seven thematic courses focusing on topics such as how to write a Data Management Plan (DMP) and how to share research data. The courses are announced on the university web portal, and all researchers, students, and administrative staff at UiT can freely attend any of the courses. All courses are delivered both in classrooms and via Skype, with Norwegian and English as the languages of instruction.

## Tips for Embedding Engagement in the Course Delivery

Helene offers the following tips for embedding engagement tactics into the courses:

1. **Provide online video-conferencing to reach people remotely**. This is especially helpful for multi-campus institutions. UiT has nine campuses across the northern part of Norway, and providing regular classroom training to all UiT staff is challenging. People find it convenient to follow the courses via video-conference (Skype, for example) and bringing together a group in this way helps to bridge the distances. However, to make the best use of video-conference technology as a teacher, it is important to practice how to deliver the course in this new way. In particular, you should become familiar with aspects such as sharing screens, using desktop applications, and being comfortable with talking to people who are only present via a camera.

5 Open Courses at UiT Library, http://site.uit.no/rdmtraining/course-info/?lang=en/

2. **Keep the courses short and focused**. All UiT open courses are limited to 45 minutes and focus on specific topics so as not to overload participants.

3. **Make the course interactive**; using a variety of teaching materials helps. A selection of thematic RDM issues are currently being recorded as separate instruction videos that will be made available online. This will make it possible to adjust the balance of the course: by asking participants to watch selected videos before coming to the course, more time can be devoted to activities and discussions.

4. **Keep the content of the course up-to-date**. The team pays attention to emerging subjects, such as the European General Data Protection Regulation (GDPR), or data processing agreements, and regularly incorporates new topics into the course. Helene explains: 'We actively seek out the gaps in the course series, as it should eventually reflect the entire RDM life cycle.'

5. **Use all channels at your disposal to promote the course**. The RDM training at UiT is presented in a central portal, containing all the necessary course information, calendar of dates, and much more. The team use social media channels, mailing lists, personal contacts at the faculties and, of course, rely on the message being spread by word of mouth. Key individuals such as subject librarians (specialised librarians in certain disciplines) are also encouraged to send information to their networks.

6. **Do not just *think about* engagement: start doing it**. This is especially crucial for large institutions with multiple campuses. The UiT RDM team is based on only one campus, but regularly goes on 'Open Science Tours' to other campuses. The team uses these tours as an opportunity to talk to campus managers and local library staff, provide courses, and generally to make themselves visible to colleagues on different campuses.

Since the introduction of the open courses, there has been an increasing proportion of researchers among the attendees, relative to administrative staff. This could indicate a cultural change across the institution, and an increasing appreciation of RDM principles among researchers.

Helene offers a final tip to those interested in implementing a similar initiative: 'Don't wait too long until you get going. You don't need a full-scale plan, just start with what you have. We have learned a lot simply by meeting people.'

event
data
RDM
Maria
time
also
theme
engage
says
one
open
two
best
Share
talk
call
Fig
well
staff
together
just
put
can
focus
it's
took
peers
place
first
course
Dan
Teperek

# 4. Dedicated Events to Gauge Interest and Build Networks

Humans are social animals, so physical events are a good vehicle with which to engage people. Who doesn't like to go to concerts, gigs or exhibitions? Unsurprisingly, librarians have capitalised on people's natural affinity for a get-together. Five different European libraries started using dedicated events to encourage research communities to be interested in data management and to create engagement, and the idea for such events is spreading.

Two cases: the 'Dealing with Data' conference at the University of Edinburgh and 'DuoDi — Days of Data' from Vilnius University, describe how to engage with researchers by organising events promoting tools and services for data management.

The remaining cases, 'Data Conversations' from Lancaster University, which has also been implemented at Vrije University Amsterdam and at the Open University, discusses informal events — by researchers, for researchers. The conversations are organised around data management topics which appeal to the research community.

Bigger events, such as the 'Dealing with Data' conference, tend to be more time-consuming to organise and also more costly. Informal events are typically less time-consuming and less costly to organise, particularly if they are not part of a recurring series, and therefore easier to adapt at other institutions.

# 4.1. 'Dealing with Data' Conference at the University of Edinburgh

*Author: Elli Papadopoulou*

*Contributor: Kerry Miller*

***University of Edinburgh staff organise an annual conference and create internal forums for researchers to talk about research data.***

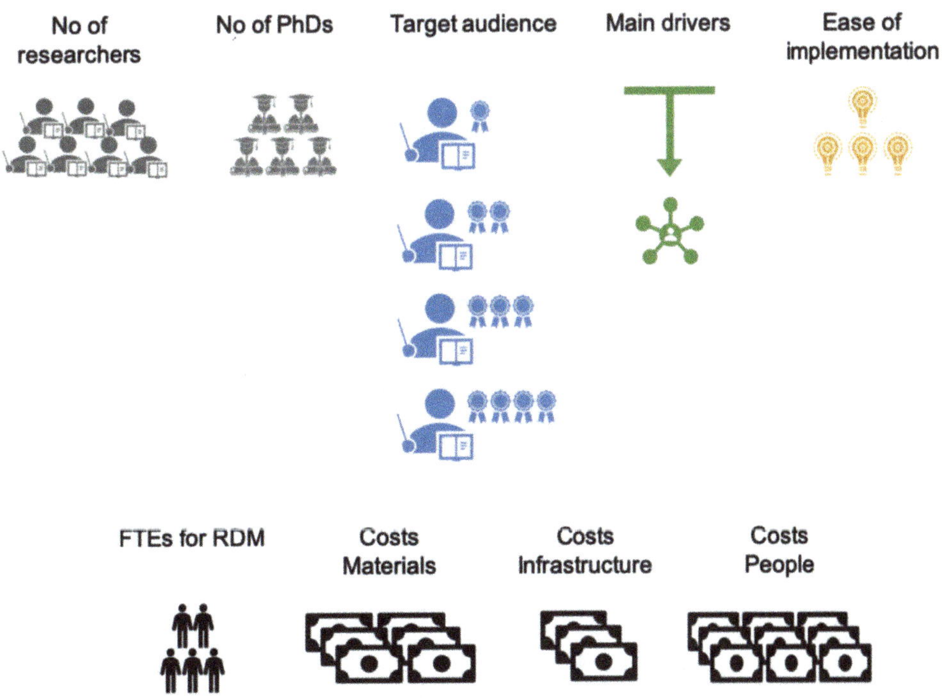


Table 4.1, CC BY 4.0.


https://doi.org/10.11647/OBP.0185.10

Fig. 4.1 A collage from the 'Dealing with Data' conference 2018 by Robin Rice. © University of Edinburgh 2018, CC BY 4.0.

## Inviting Researchers to Explain How *They* Deal with Data

It is indisputable that in order to successfully engage with researchers, you need to understand what is important to them, and be able to 'speak their language'. So what better way to gain this understanding than putting them in the spotlight and giving them the microphone? That's exactly what the University of Edinburgh Library[1] did: they established an annual conference to give researchers an opportunity to share their own data experiences both with their peers and with library staff.

'"Dealing with Data" is our annual showcase event. It gives researchers a valuable opportunity to discuss their research data challenges and solutions, while also improving the visibility of the services we provide and allowing us to make new contacts within our

1 University of Edinburgh Library website, https://www.ed.ac.uk/information-services/library-museum-gallery

research communities,' says Kerry Miller, the Research Data Support Officer, Library & University Collections, The University of Edinburgh.

## Hunting for a Good Theme

Every year the library looks for a theme for the data conference, based on international, European and/or national developments. The aim is to find a theme that will ensure inspiring presentations and therefore lead to engagement and discussions.[2] This year's theme is 'collaboration and solutions about sharing and re-using data'.

Once the theme is selected, the library reaches out to faculties to identify researchers who have experience related to that theme, and who would either like to be a keynote speaker or to make a statement on specific aspects of the theme. Having selected main contributors and put a preliminary programme in place, an official call for contributions is sent through the library's communication channels.

## Manoeuvring to Broaden the Audience

There are, however, still research groups that don't engage with Research Data Management (RDM). 'On the one hand we have some researchers who are enthusiastic about data and want to talk more about what they are doing and how they are doing it, and on the other, we see a lack of interest from some researchers,' admits Kerry.

The library tries to find alternative ways to engage with uninterested researchers and to encourage them to come to the conference, reaching out through their contacts within the schools. Approaching researchers through their peers, rather than via Information Services, helps to persuade them of the relevance of the subject.

Usually though, just giving researchers the opportunity to present their own work is enough to attract their participation, and to attract the attention of their peers. The popularity of the event demonstrates its success: 100–150 participants each time and still growing.

---

2 To get a better idea of the structure around the theme, you may consult past Dealing with Data programmes for 2018 and 2017 at the University of Edinburgh Media Hopper Create space, 'Dealing with Data Conferences', https://media.ed.ac.uk/channel/Dealing+With+Data+2017+Conference/82256222

# 4.2. DuoDi: The 'Days of Data' at Vilnius University

*Author: Elli Papadopoulou*

*Contributor: Ramutė Grabauskienė*

***Vilnius University engages with researchers about RDM through the effective promotion of a month of structured mini-events teaching best practice.***

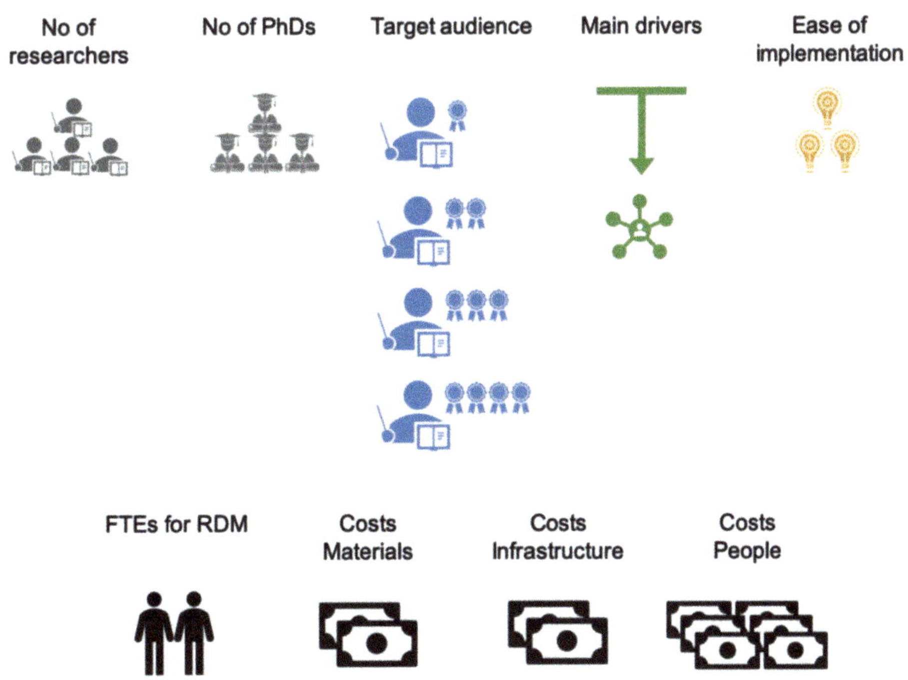


Table 4.2, CC BY 4.0.

 https://doi.org/10.11647/OBP.0185.11

## Library Services from a Business Perspective

In the commercial world, enterprises develop products and services, then promote them to customers to facilitate wide adoption and uptake. Similarly, libraries have a pool of resources and services developed to support researchers, so why not promote them in the way that a business person would? That was the thinking that drove Vilnius University Library to build a community around their Research Data Management (RDM) support service.[3]

Their promotion took the form of five mini-events over the course of a month, called 'DuoDi'[4] (an abbreviation of '**Duo**menų **Di**enos' or 'Days of Data', which creates an acronym meaning 'to give' in Lithuanian).

Each mini-event was a training workshop in three phases:

1. ACCEPT — increase participants' familiarity with the RDM support and resources available at the library, including data management planning;
2. ACT — learn how to use the National Open Access Research Data Archive, MIDAS,[5] and its data analysis tool DAMIS;[6]
3. BREAK THROUGH — publish and share research data.

## Success and the Need to Grow

The 'Days of Data' events were initiated after recognizing that researchers needed RDM support, and that the demand was increasing because Data Management Plans (DMPs) had become a requirement for research proposals submitted to in response to national calls in Lithuania. To address this growing demand for support, the Vilnius University Library organised 'Days of Data' in collaboration with one of the faculties.

'Days of Data' sessions last two hours and cover best practices in writing DMPs, as well as more theoretical issues around RDM. 'The approach has been much more effective [than previous approaches],

3 Vilnius University Library RDM, https://biblioteka.vu.lt/en/science-and-studies/scholarly-communication/research-data-management

4 DuoDi events, https://www.midas.lt/public-app.html#/news?documentId=100681&newFields=Body&galleryField=GalleryImage&titleField=Title&lang=en

5 MIDAS data archive, https://www.midas.lt/public-app.html#/midas?lang=en

6 DAMIS data analysis tool, https://damis.midas.lt/login.html

but requires effort to prepare the specific examples needed for different scientific disciplines each time, as well as to promote the event through multiple communication channels: we even reach out to the Public Relations Office!' explains Ramutė Grabauskienė, former Data Manager.

She recognises the wider impact of the 'Days of Data': 'Some researchers have already uploaded their data to the repository, however, sometimes they are not willing to openly share their data with others; there's still work to do,' and she can cite cases when people have come to the library after the events looking for further support.

The 'Days of Data' have been a start, but they are just one of the mechanisms by which the team at Vilnius hopes to increase engagement with researchers and develop knowledge. Ramutė presents their plans: 'One of the things we are looking into at the moment, for example, is not only organising these group activities that take place at one moment during the year, but arranging individual consultations and personal meetings with researchers to truly increase researcher engagement.'

# 4.3. Let's Talk Data: Data Conversations at Lancaster University

*Author: Marta Teperek*

*Contributor: Joshua Sendall and Hardy Schwamm*

***Researchers at Lancaster University build an RDM community of practice through informal events on research data with multiple speakers and plenty of discussion time.***

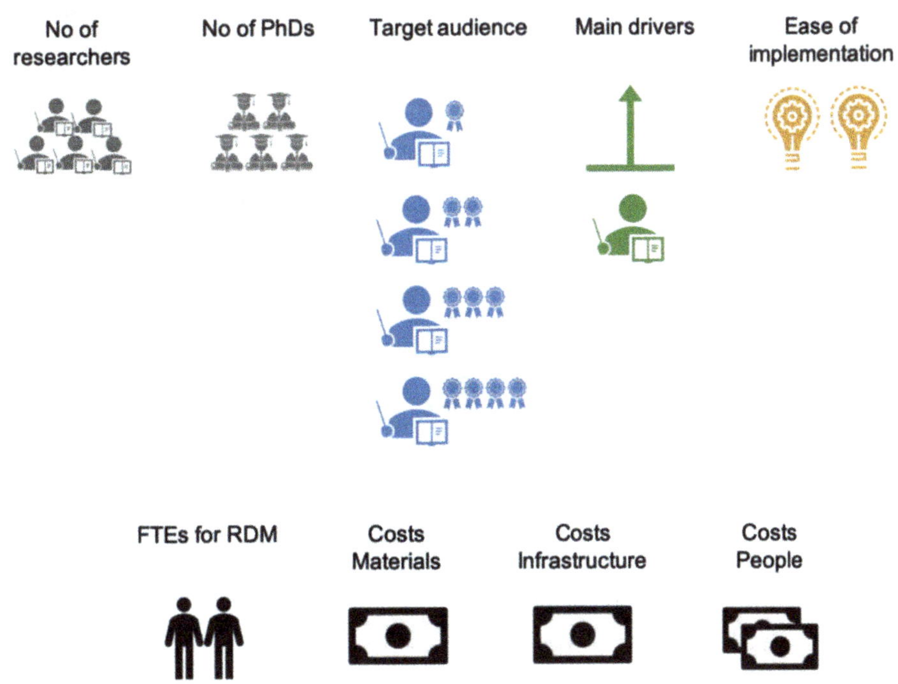


Table 4.3, CC BY 4.0.

 https://doi.org/10.11647/OBP.0185.12

## Little Time? Little Money?... But Still Want to Have a Community of Researchers Talking with Passion about Data? You Can Have It with Data Conversations!

Lancaster University started their Data Conversations initiative with the belief that to improve data management practice, they needed to turn away from policy-driven approaches and address cultural issues instead.

Data Conversations are informal, lunchtime talks with time for discussion, which channel researchers' passions to focus on the human aspects of Research Data Management (RDM). 'They bring research data stories to life,' says Joshua Sendall, Research Data Manager and the organiser of Data Conversations at Lancaster. 'An approach which communicates the intrinsic value of RDM best practice seems to be a better vehicle to drive people to best practices than one which mandates compliance,' he reasons.

Fig. 4.2 Joshua Sendall, Research Data Manager at Lancaster University. © Joshua Sendall, CC BY 4.0.

## So What's the Recipe?

It is simple: book a nice venue, invite speakers, order pizzas, advertise the event and sit back and let researchers do the talking. Joshua estimates that it takes about two-and-a-half days to organise such an event. He admits that, in practice, the event promotion can be time-consuming. In addition, it's important to think carefully about the topic: subjects that appeal to a broad range of researchers will attract a more diverse audience from a broader group of disciplines. Of course, a catchy title always helps!

## If You Want to Talk about Data, Allow Time for Talking

To increase the diversity of views, each Data Conversation has at least four speakers. Lancaster identifies the speakers in two ways: 'if we already know about an expert on the topic, we will approach them,' explains Joshua, 'but then there is also the open call — when people sign up for the data conversation, they can sign up either to attend or to speak.'

About fifty percent of the speakers are invited, while the other half is identified through the open call. The presentations typically take no longer than 10 minutes and are followed by lively and dynamic discussions. 'We strive to provide enough time for discussions, so there are always long breaks timetabled between the talks,' adds Joshua.

## Community Building and Cultural Change

Lancaster University Library organises Data Conversations twice a year and has already held 7 events with almost 240 attendees in total. Some of the PhD students who had been attending Data Conversations from the beginning have now graduated and moved on. 'It's nice to know that they are embarking on their careers with the awareness of open data and good RDM,' reflects Joshua.

But does the initiative really lead to cultural change? Joshua sends out a survey after each event and the feedback has been positive, but he prefers to focus on qualitative measures. 'Researchers said that Data Conversations have changed their practice and we've seen it act as an interdisciplinary incubator,' he says. Data Conversations bring people together from various disciplines. 'This is where our investment pays dividends: in the relationships developed through these conversations. And there is a sense of community as well,' reflects Joshua.

Data Conversations have also acted as a springboard for other initiatives. Due to the interest that the attendees expressed in open research, Lancaster has now started a new initiative, 'Open Research Café'. In addition, they recently partnered with researchers from the Department of Psychology at Lancaster to run a full-day workshop on open research based on the Data Conversations model.

## 'FAIL' Means 'First Attempt In Learning'

While the initiative is relatively easy to implement, Joshua warns: 'Be mindful that initiatives such as Data Conversations can take some time to gain traction. Building a brand and awareness takes time.' Joshua also thinks organisers shouldn't be afraid of failure. Laughing, he says that in Lancaster they remind themselves of the saying 'FAIL means First Attempt In Learning'. 'You learn from experience, and put a different spin on things which didn't work,' he adds.

Joshua always approaches the day of the event with a degree of nervousness and apprehension. He wonders if things will go to plan, if people will turn up, if pizzas will arrive. However, he reflects, 'once the event is taking place, you put all those apprehensions aside and you become lost in the event and you realise, that's it, it has been a success!'

## Additional Resources

- Information about the Data Conversations initiative from the University of Lancaster, https://www.lancaster.ac.uk/library/rdm/data-conversations/
- Blog post by Maria Cruz who attended one of the Data Conversations events: 'Building Connections through Data Conversations at Lancaster University', 28 February 2019, https://www.rd-alliance.org/blogs/building-connections-through-data-conversations-lancaster-university.html-0
- Research support news from the Lancaster University Library, 'Highly Relevant', http://wp.lancs.ac.uk/highly-relevant/

# 4.4. Starting New Data Conversations at Vrije Universiteit Amsterdam

*Author: Marta Teperek*

*Contributor: Maria Cruz*

***Staff at Vrije Universiteit Amsterdam reflect on the benefits and challenges of starting an RDM community of practice through informal researcher-led events.***

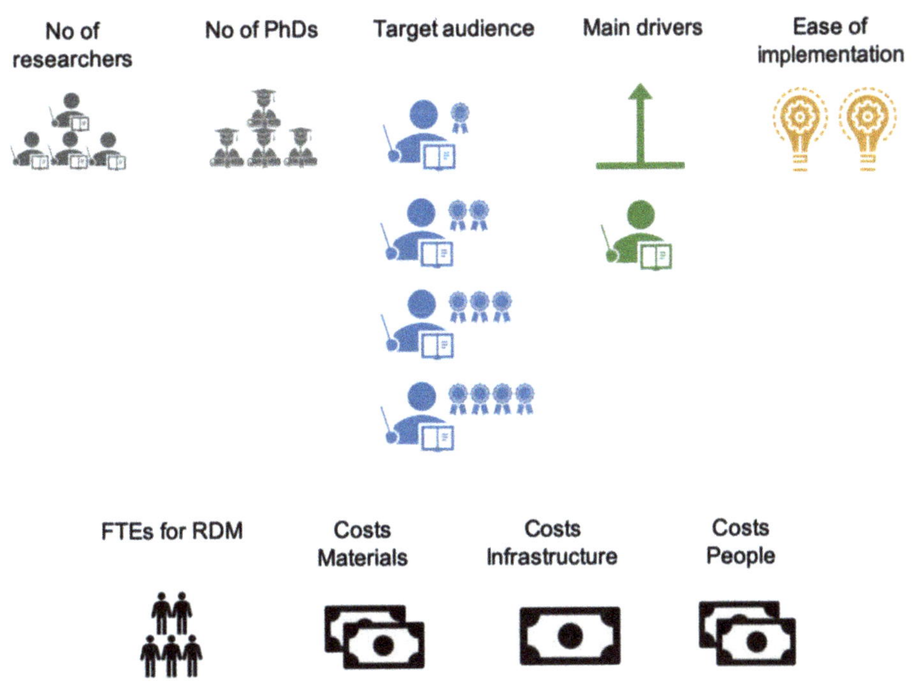


Table 4.4, CC BY 4.0.


https://doi.org/10.11647/OBP.0185.13

'We wanted to build a community of researchers interested in data, but we didn't know where to start and had only limited resources,' says Maria Cruz, Community Manager RDM at Vrije Universiteit Amsterdam (VU). She attended one of Lancaster's Data Conversations and got inspired. 'I loved that it was researcher-led: researchers had lively RDM conversations and kept answering each other's questions on the subject. It was impressive. I loved the concept and seeing it in action made me want to start this at the VU.'

## Getting the Timing Right

The VU had an impressive start. Close to 40 people attended the first event, which was a pleasant surprise given that it took time to build such an audience at Lancaster. Maria thinks that shortening the event to one-and-a-half hours might have helped: 'one-and-a-half hours isn't much longer than an extended lunch break;' however, she warns: 'ensuring diversity, having at least four 10-minute talks lined up, plus allowing 15 minutes at the beginning for lunch, plus time for discussion, means that scheduling and chairing is tricky. It's always a pity to interrupt animated discussions between researchers.'

## Good Connections Mean a Lot

Maria also reflected that the administrative effort to put the event together took her only two days. She believes it's thanks to their existing strong networks. The VU already had good connections with PhD students developed through previous training, which meant less effort spent on advertising. Maria also already knew some influencers from previous events and she could send them personal invitations and ask them to distribute the message. 'These are people whose emails will translate into registrations,' she says.

## An Engaging Event Is Not the Same as Community Building

Maria emphasised that it's important to manage expectations. 'Putting the event together is not demanding, but a community doesn't grow by itself — it requires resources and time.' People come to an event and then they go away. Keeping track of those who attend these events and staying in touch with them can facilitate community building, but it requires additional effort and careful planning.

Fig. 4.3 Q&A session during a data event. © Jan van der Heul/TU Delft, CC BY 4.0.

## Keep Calm and Get Started

Contemplating starting Data Conversations at your institution? 'Attend one if it's nearby, talk to people who organised it; seeing it happen and chatting with people is inspiring and helps to get started,' says Maria. She believes that as long as you have a gut feeling that Data Conversations could work at your institution, you should go for it and you shouldn't get discouraged if some people are sceptical. There will be others who will share your enthusiasm!

After the first Data Conversation at the VU, a few of the attendees approached Maria and thanked her for organising the event. This, together with the positive feedback received through a feedback form, made Maria very happy and convinced that 'it was certainly worth it!'

## Additional Resources

- Information about Data Conversations at the VU, https://vu-nl.libcal.com/event/3386300
- Collection of presentations of the first event, https://doi.org/10.5281/zenodo.3251806

# 4.5. Talk to Understand Your Community Better: Informal Events at the Open University

*Author: Marta Teperek*

*Contributor: Dan Crane*

*Reflections on how informal discussion forums and speaker-led lunchtime events have helped Open University RDM engage with their research community.*

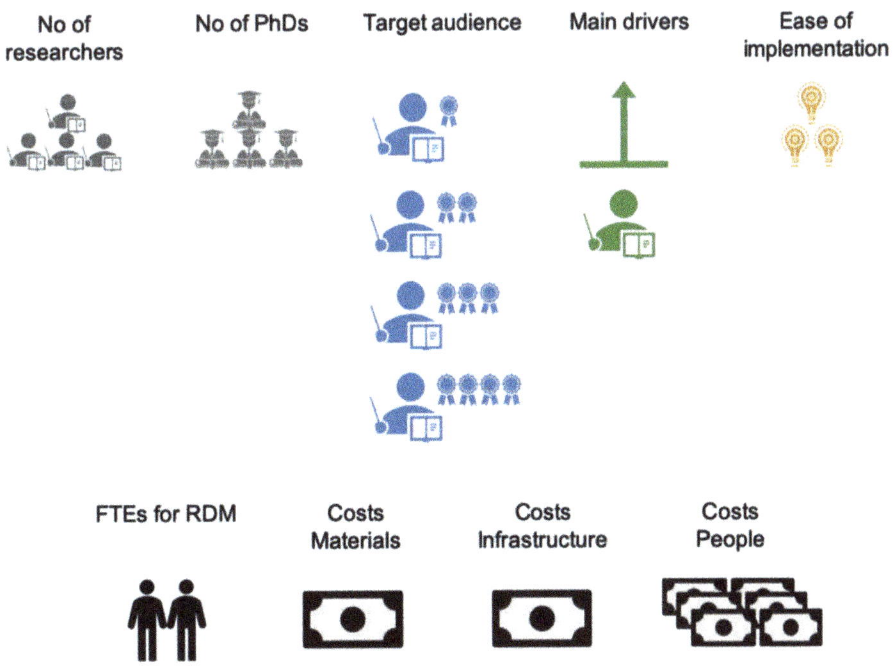


Table 4.5, CC BY 4.0.

 https://doi.org/10.11647/OBP.0185.14

The Open University (OU) in the UK used informal events as a vehicle to hear from researchers about their work and what was important to them. 'We offer RDM support through our website, training, repository and enquiries, but contact with researchers is largely limited to those who get in touch or attend our sessions. It seems natural for us to focus on the mandated and defined goals of data management planning and meeting funder requirements — they are of course important — but are they the things that are most important to researchers as well?' wonders Nicola Dowson, Senior Library Services Manager for Research Support at the OU Library.

## Two Informal Events to Get Discussions Started

'We've held two events where we invited researchers to come and talk about RDM in an informal setting, without us talking *at* them or pushing an agenda of policy compliance, or telling them why they should write a DMP,' explains Dan Crane, the librarian at the OU.

The two events were:

- 'Data Resolutions': an open discussion forum without an agenda or structure, just allowing the conversation to flow.[7]
- 'Data Conversations': a more structured lunchtime event, following the Lancaster model explored in case 4.3, with a mixture of academic staff, PhD students, and RDM staff as speakers.[8]

## So What's Next?

The OU aren't sure yet whether they will organise more events of this kind in the future. These initial discussions highlighted that research at the OU is varied; different disciplines, methods, and groups, require different solutions and approaches. This has inspired them to launch a Data Champions programme (similar to the Cambridge University model detailed in case 5.1) and a call has been issued for researchers

---

7 Data Resolutions at the OU (blog post): Dan Crane, 'Research Data Resolutions', 8 February 2018, http://www.open.ac.uk/blogs/the_orb/?p=2553

8 Data Conversations at the OU (blog post): Dan Crane, 'Data Conversation — talking with researchers about open data, 14 December 2018, http://www.open.ac.uk/blogs/the_orb/?p=3091

Fig. 4.4 Informal discussions with researchers. © Jan van der Heul/TU Delft, CC BY 4.0.

who are ready to lead by example and share best practice within their communities.[9]

## Advice for Others Who Want to Start

'Be bold and do it! Don't spend too much time thinking about whether it will work and if it will be successful. The worst result would be that not many people turn up. But just go ahead and do it. Someone will come!' says Dan. 'Seeing researchers engaged and enjoying the event makes it really worth the effort.'

9 Call for Data Champions at the OU (blog post): Isabel Chadwick, 'Call for Data Champions!', 26 June 2019, http://www.open.ac.uk/blogs/the_orb/?p=3267

Delft
WUR
support
can
within
time
Will
reward
good
staff
OSC
James
meet
build
team
Erik
Lauren
van
also
made
tasks
call
new
current
Clare
across
policy
social
units
order
learn
must
forward
measure
since
Center
experts
ways
early
part
lab
plan
plans
contact
well
counts
various
Saskia
explore
needs
local
Balázs
Bergh
Den
PhD
field
blog
read
join
arts
year
case
Fig
website
practices
drive
FTE
Team
make
every
written
der
Make
one
use

# 5. Networks of Data Champions

Good Research Data Management (RDM) practice can be challenging to achieve in higher education institutions because of the diverse nature of the research community. Difficulties also arise because researchers may not possess the skills, resources or time to manage their research data effectively; they may not be aware of the benefits of RDM and open science; or perhaps they don't see its value since it is not well incentivised by the current academic system. Many institutions have already implemented centralised research data management units to mitigate such problems and provide support, but the desired discipline-specific expertise, and the resources required for training, remain limited.

## Lack of Funding? Need More RDM Support? Build a Community-Based Model

Implementing a network of Data Champions can provide a cost-effective solution to improve RDM support. Essentially, Data Champions are individuals who volunteer their discipline-specific expertise; they lead by example to promote FAIR (Findable, Accessible, Interoperable, Re-usable) data principles, advocate good RDM practice and advise members of their local research community on the proper handling of research data. They use their passion for knowledge exchange and desire to build a collaborative and researcher-led community to drive the uptake of open science principles in their departments and institutes, and engage with central RDM units to improve understanding of research practices in their discipline.

Fig. 5. The definition of a TU Delft Data Champion. © Connie Clare/TU Delft, CC BY 4.0.

In this chapter we share success stories and valuable lessons learned from research institutes that have pioneered the development of community-based models in order to better engage researchers with research data. We learn how to establish a Data Champions community from the University of Cambridge, how to reward and recognise Data Champions from TU Delft, and how to launch a similar Data Stewards programme from Wageningen University.

# 5.1. Data Champion Programme at the University of Cambridge

*Author: Connie Clare*

*Contributors: Lauren Cadwallader, Sacha Jones, James Savage*

***The University of Cambridge links central RDM support to a network of volunteer Data Champions to efficiently disseminate RDM knowledge and training, start conversations across research units, and gather discipline-specific expertise for input on policy.***

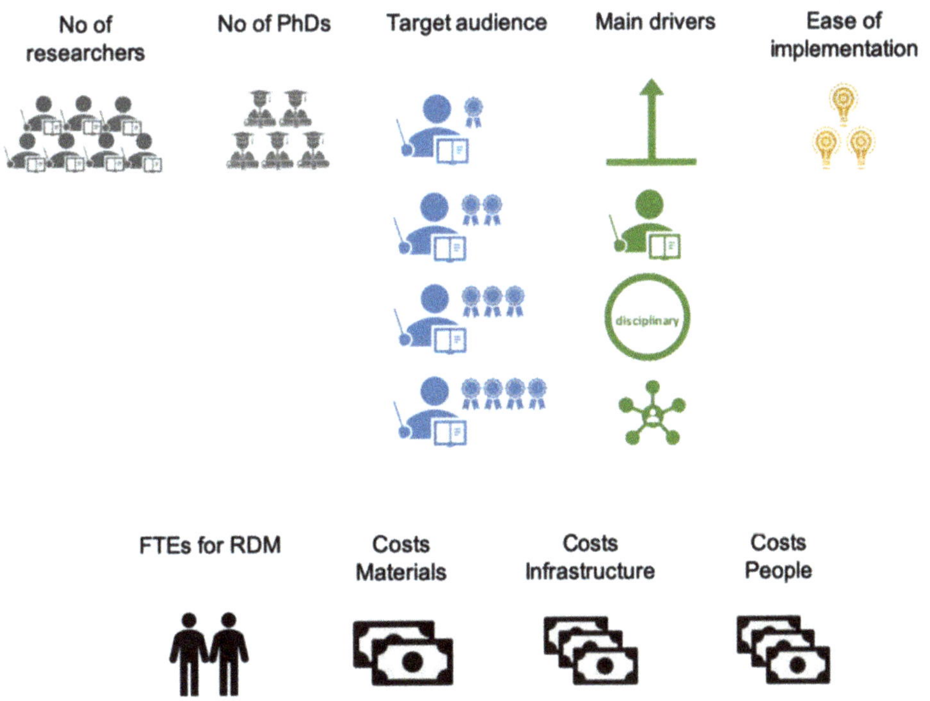


Table 5.1, CC BY 4.0.

 https://doi.org/10.11647/OBP.0185.15

## Establishing a Data Champions Network

The University of Cambridge kick-started their Data Champion programme[1] in September 2016 to drive cultural change towards open data within 6 academic schools and around 100 departments and institutes across the university. The programme is centrally coordinated by the Research Data Management Facility in the Office of Scholarly Communication (OSC).[2]

The OSC provides information about good Research Data Management (RDM) practice, short training courses, consultancy, and guidance for researchers depositing their data in the institutional repository, but it cannot meet demand. Lauren Cadwallader, Deputy Head of Scholarly Communication and manager of the Research Data Management Facility, explains how establishing the Data Champions network has helped the OSC to meet these growing research demands. 'Without our Data Champions it would be physically impossible for the OSC to reach the many thousands of researchers at the University.' With only two employees, who each spend about 0.3 FTE (Full-Time Equivalent) of their time coordinating the programme, Lauren reveals that 'embedding Data Champions within many schools and departments has dramatically extended the influence of the OSC in promoting the open science agenda across a breadth of research disciplines.'

## Growth of a Community

Since its inception, the University of Cambridge Data Champion programme has made three successive calls for volunteers. Following the most recent call made in January 2019, the programme comprises an impressive 87 active members.[3] This substantial cohort of Data Champions welcomes anyone interested in data management, including researchers (from early to established), technicians, data managers, IT professionals, librarians and data scientists. The programme also includes 'affiliated' Data Champions, who are individuals who contribute their RDM expertise without working to benefit any specific department.

---

1 Cambridge Data Champions, https://www.data.cam.ac.uk/intro-data-champions

2 Cambridge Research Data Management, https://www.data.cam.ac.uk/

3 Members of the Cambridge Data Champions community, https://www.data.cam.ac.uk/data-champions-search

Image removed due to possible license restrictions

Fig. 5.1 A cartoon advertising the Data Champions network at the University of Cambridge. © Clare Trowell/University of Cambridge, CC BY-NC-ND.

## What Does It Take to Become a Data Champion?

The first call for volunteers (September 2016), outlined the various roles and responsibilities of prospective Data Champions, requesting that they act as local experts and advocates for good RDM, serve as RDM representatives by attending bimonthly forums, forward questions to the RDM team, and conduct at least one workshop per year. However, as the programme evolved it became apparent that the first cohort of Data Champions were delivering RDM support and advocacy in a variety of ways, from writing data management plans to conducting electronic lab notebook trials, but not necessarily by conducting a workshop. Consequently, the second call (February 2018) was amended such that Data Champions were not required to deliver any particular type of support.[4]

4 'Cambridge Data Champions — reflections on an expanding community and

## What's in It for You?

Becoming a Data Champion has many benefits. Lauren highlights the opportunity to enhance professional development through the programme. 'Many individuals join the team to learn new skills and improve their own RDM practice.' She adds, 'by undertaking OSC training and organising extracurricular activities, individuals can develop essential transferable skills to boost their CV and future career prospects.'

Joining the vibrant community of Data Champions can facilitate multidisciplinary collaboration with like-minded personnel, increase an individual's impact beyond their immediate circle, and present opportunities for networking beyond the University. This was wonderfully demonstrated by Data Champion and postdoctoral researcher from the Department of Zoology, James Savage, who received funding through the OSC to attend the International Data Week 2018[5] conference in Botswana and gave a presentation on the Data Champion Programme. James embraced this opportunity by engaging with representatives of similar programmes at the conference, disseminating the knowledge he gained back to the Data Champion programme, and ultimately publishing a practice paper[6] to summarise the progress made on the establishment of the Data Champion community at the University of Cambridge.

## The Challenges

Whilst establishing a community of Data Champions provides many benefits, there are also many challenges. The main issues revolve around: (i) attracting new volunteers, in particular from the arts, humanities and social sciences; (ii) sustaining motivation and productivity amongst the existing cohort; (iii) maintaining central support; and, (iv) providing incentives to devote time to the programme.

---

strategies for 2019' (blog post), 19 June 2019, https://unlockingresearch-blog.lib.cam.ac.uk/?p=2602

5 Information about the International Data Week, https://internationaldataweek.org/

6 J. L. Savage and L. Cadwallader, 'Establishing, Developing, and Sustaining a Community of Data Champions,' *Data Science Journal* 18:1 (2019), 23, https://datascience.codata.org/articles/10.5334/dsj-2019-023/

James emphasised the additional problem of bias towards STEM (Science, Technology, Engineering, and Mathematics) disciplines in the current demographic of Data Champions (since only 18% of current Data Champions work in humanities and social science disciplines, with none in the arts). To address this problem, the language of the most recent call was altered to make it more inclusive to individuals working within those disciplines. James stressed the importance of promoting diversity and inclusion when establishing a community of Data Champions. 'The programme was designed for all disciplines. All researchers should have a voice to direct the future of the Data Champion programme at the University of Cambridge.'

# 5.2. TU Delft Data Champions

*Author: Connie Clare*

*Contributor: Yasemin Türkyilmaz-van der Velden*

***RDM staff at TU Delft reflect on the value of their network of volunteer Data Champions for engaging with the research community, and explore how Data Champions can be appropriately rewarded for their contributions.***

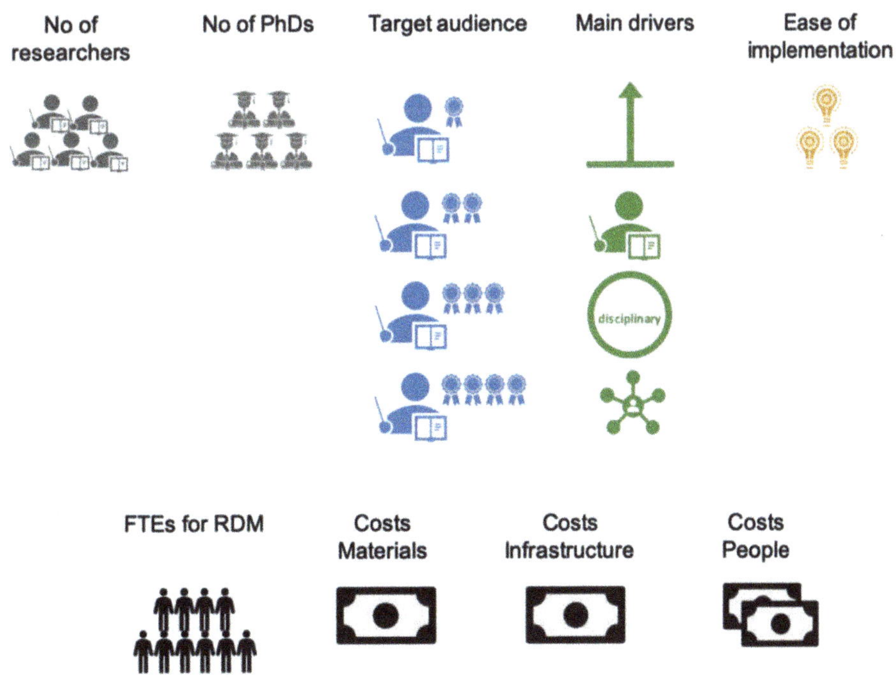


Table 5.2, CC BY 4.0.

 https://doi.org/10.11647/OBP.0185.16

Inspired by the original University of Cambridge Data Champions programme, TU Delft Data Champions programme was launched in September 2018 to deliver disciplinary-specific support to all 8 research faculties of Delft University of Technology. Sharing the common goal of advocating proper Research Data Management (RDM) practice, both programmes adopt a centrally-coordinated, researcher-led and bottom-up approach to community building.

As described in case 6.1, TU Delft Data Stewards are full-time staff embedded within each faculty with the purpose of being the first point of contact for inquiries relating to RDM practice. However, it is appreciated that Data Stewards will not possess all of the disciplinary experience and will not have all of the answers all of the time. Furthermore, they are unable to reach every single researcher; therefore there is a need for Data Champions to build on the existing infrastructure to create a cohesive web of support.

## The Glue that Holds the Community Together

Data Champions are a valuable asset to the TU Delft research community. To date, there are 47 Champions and numbers are continually increasing. Data Steward and Data Champion Community Manager, Yasemin Türkyilmaz-van der Velden, tells us how the programme responds to the needs of Data Champions so that they can cater to the needs of their community: 'We appreciate that Data Champions are volunteers who offer their time, support and expertise out of goodwill. As this is not their full-time position and because time is in short supply, we don't enforce strict requirements on what they must deliver. Rather, we give them the flexibility to make their individual contribution to the community of TU Delft as they wish.'

## Reward and Recognition: If They Make It 'FAIR' for Us, We Should Make It Fair for Them

One of the key objectives at TU Delft is to reward the exemplary efforts of their Data Champions by giving them more publicity, which in turn can raise their professional profile. Many researchers

Fig. 5.2 The network of Data Champions meet to discuss ideas and share knowledge at TU Delft. © Jan van der Heul/TU Delft, CC BY 4.0.

are taking great leaps forward to advance open science by making their data 'FAIR' (Findable Accessible Interoperable and Re-usable) but are not widely recognised for their inspiring work. TU Delft want to commend their Data Champions and express gratitude to those who go the extra mile.

A recent internship project is currently underway to publicise the achievements of TU Delft's Data Champions. One-to-one interviews are conducted with Champions to learn more about their research projects, how they effectively engage with researchers, their motivations for becoming Data Champions, and their future goals and aspirations. Following each interview, each Data Champion case study is written and published as an article on TU Delft's 'Open Working' blog (alongside a quirky illustration), under a dedicated tab on the Homepage titled 'Data Champions'.[7] Here are examples of articles written to showcase their stories:

7 Data Champions page on the Open Working blog, https://openworking.wordpress.com/data-champions/

- 'The Changing Landscape of Open Geospatial Data', 10 July 2019 — Balázs Dukai harnesses the power of existing data to build 3D city models[8]
- 'Keep calm and go paperless: Electronic lab notebooks can improve your research', 5 July 2019 — Siân Jones champions the use of Electronic Lab Notebooks[9]
- 'Reduce, Reuse, Recycle knowledge: How open hardware can help to build a more sustainable future', 3 July 2019 — José Carlos Urra Llanusa shares his vision of open hardware,[10]
- 'Can I really read your emotions if I look deep into your eyes', 2 July 2019 — Joost de Winter explains the importance of replication research in the field of 'Cognitive Robotics'[11]

## Tweeting and Tagging

Articles and events are regularly published and shared to the blog and social media accounts (for example, Twitter, LinkedIn and Slack) in order to increase the visibility of the Data Champions programme. Making the Data Champion network more transparent online facilitates community interaction and incentivises a wider community to engage with the programme. This may be particularly important to demonstrate the benefits of the programme to those who might be reluctant to join because they fear that becoming a Data Champion will place added burdens on them, in addition to their other academic commitments.

8 'The Changing Landscape of Open Geospatial Data', https://openworking.wordpress.com/2019/07/10/the-changing-landscape-of-open-geospatial-data/

9 'Keep calm and go paperless: Electronic lab notebooks can improve your research', https://openworking.wordpress.com/2019/07/05/keep-calm-and-go-paperless-electronic-lab-notebooks-can-improve-your-research/

10 'Reduce, Reuse, Recycle knowledge: How open hardware can help to build a more sustainable future', https://openworking.wordpress.com/2019/07/03/reduce-reuse-recycle-knowledge-how-open-hardware-can-help-to-build-a-more-sustainable-future/

11 'Can I really read your emotions if I look deep into your eyes', https://openworking.wordpress.com/2019/07/02/can-i-really-read-your-emotions-if-i-look-deep-into-your-eyes/

## Final Thoughts and Future Steps

Yasemin stimulates further debate over the best way to reward, recognise and incentivise good RDM practice in her final thoughts on the matter. 'To successfully sustain a thriving community of Data Champions at TU Delft we must continue to reward their efforts and explore innovative ways of reinventing the programme to attract new Data Champions and maintain turnover.'

In a recent interview with TU Delft library, Balázs Dukai expressed his feelings of personal satisfaction and accomplishment upon joining the network of Data Champions. 'As an individual researcher, becoming a Data Champion has allowed me to acquire valuable skills and knowledge that I wouldn't have otherwise encountered. As part of a wider research community, becoming a Data Champion has allowed me to connect my group with a diverse network with opportunity for collaboration.' From this we conclude that whilst efforts should be made to reward and recognise Data Champions for their work, simply becoming a member of a supportive community network can be a reward in itself.

# 5.3. Data Stewards at Wageningen University and Research

*Author: Connie Clare*

*Contributors: Saskia van Marrewijk and Erik van Den Bergh*

***Wageningen University's network of Data Stewards will be formed primarily from existing academic and research-related staff given new formal roles and responsibilities around supporting RDM.***

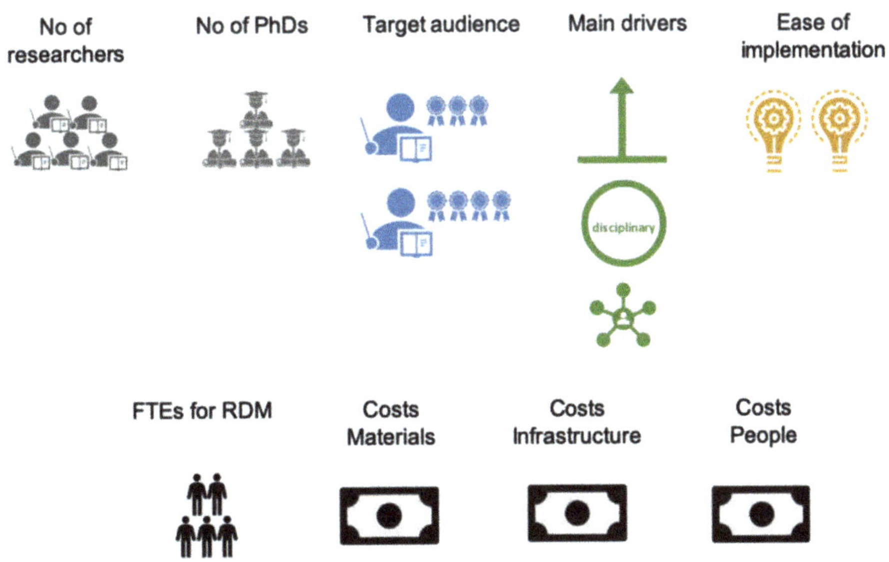


Table 5.3, CC BY 4.0.

 https://doi.org/10.11647/OBP.0185.17

The Wageningen Data Competency Center (WDCC) was established at Wageningen University and Research (WUR) in September 2017 to support developments in the field of big data. The Center encompasses five WUR policy lines: (1) education, (2) research, (3) data management, (4) infrastructure, and (5) value creation, to integrate and strengthen the existing organisation of education and research within the University.

## Meet the Team

The Data Management Support Team, a collaboration of WUR Library and IT (Information Technology), coordinated by the WDCC, comprises 9 employees from the library, legal services and IT, who provide guidance for researchers throughout the research lifecycle. Additionally, the WDCC data management website[12] is a useful resource where PhD candidates can read WUR data policy[13] and regulations. What's more, researchers can contact the 'Data Desk'[14] via an open mailbox to have all of their data questions answered by a member of the support team.

## From 'Data Savvy' to 'Data Steward'

It seems as though WUR have all bases covered when it comes to helping researchers engage with their data. However, following the recent establishment of the WDCC, the major reform on EU General Data Protection Regulation (GDPR), and the amendment to WUR Data Policy that stipulates all PhD researchers must archive the data underlying their publications (as well as write a data management plan), there is increasing pressure on researchers to incorporate sustainable data management in their workflows to meet the requirements of research institutes, funding bodies and publishers alike.

The WDCC realises that one centralised support team alone will be insufficient to meet these requirements within all 6 graduate schools at WUR and have, therefore, decided to implement a community of Data

---

12 WDCC, https://www.wur.nl/en/Value-Creation-Cooperation/WDCC/Data-Management-WDCC.htm

13 WUR data policy, https://www.wur.nl/en/Value-Creation-Cooperation/WDCC/Data-Management-WDCC/Data-policy.htm

14 WUR Data Desk, https://www.wur.nl/en/Value-Creation-Cooperation/WDCC/Data-Desk.htm

Stewards to more effectively engage with their research community about data and to provide better Research Data Management (RDM) support for researchers.

According to WDDC Data Management Secretary, Saskia van Marrewijk, 'a WUR Data Steward will fulfil a similar role to that of the Data Champion at the University of Cambridge or TU Delft in the sense that they are volunteers with discipline-specific experience in good RDM practice.' She continues, 'however, at WUR we will formalise the roles and responsibilities of Data Stewards as we expect them to complete specific tasks within their research departments.'

WDCC Infrastructure Coordinator, Erik van Den Bergh, adds, 'we haven't yet appointed Data Stewards within departments but they already exist as "data-savvy personnel" working within their various departments at WUR.' Indeed, there are approximately 120 employees who frequently undertake RDM tasks as part of their daily work at WUR. 'Finally being able to award these data experts the official title of "Data Steward" means that they will be recognised for their efforts,' says Erik. 'More importantly, they will be allocated specific time to undertake RDM tasks that counts towards their working hours instead of them having to find time to complete tasks.' The WDCC anticipates that Data Stewards will dedicate time accounting for around 0.2 FTE (Full-Time Equivalent) for every 30 researchers within their departments.

Another unique aspect of the WUR Data Stewards programme is that a Data Steward position may not be available to everyone. Erik hopes that the position will be filled by established staff members, such as senior researchers, lab assistants and technicians, who have long-term employment contracts in order to avoid the risk of Data Stewards leaving with their acquired knowledge. He also believes that the position would be too laborious and time-consuming for an early career researcher. Again, this represents a very different approach to those taken by the University of Cambridge and TU Delft to build their networks of Data Champions.

## Measuring Cultural Change

Aside from basic counts of the number of visitors to the WDCC data website, the data management support team don't currently measure whether their contributions are driving cultural change within the WUR research community. However, they hope that by empowering so many staff members to advocate good data management practices, researchers will become more engaged with data topics. The WDCC is eager to measure the impacts of implementing a Data Stewards programme and plans to achieve this by using Change Performance Indicators implemented as part of their university-wide, strategic, three-year plan that was presented earlier this year. These indicators are metrics used to assess the effectiveness of the programme in improving RDM practice across WUR.

Data
data
Lab
help
need
Delft
good
Tech
new
says
one
also
Coordinator
Alastair
manager
needs
cultural
work
get
Yan
talk
way
make
three
right
well
pool
really
hired
job
skills
ability
think
Table
role
focus
act
Fig
cases
large
former
contribute
willing
multiple
success
advise
expert
study
goal
fact
use
can
will
say
want
daily
model
sheep
look
key
PhD
Person
Pronk
tasks
team
meet
it's
across
entire
order
set
able
take

# 6. Dedicated Consultants to Offer One-to-One Support with Data

What if you have slightly more resources available and would like to effectively engage with researchers across all disciplines? We recommend you consider hiring dedicated domain experts who could offer in-depth, one-to-one support to your researchers.

We collected three slightly different case studies illustrating this approach:

- Data Stewards at TU Delft;
- Informatics Lab at Virginia Tech;
- Data Managers at Utrecht University.

## Subject-Specific Consultants Are an Add-On to 'Traditional' RDM Support at Large Institutions

In all of these approaches, people who provide the consultancy support are hired full-time to do this job. In all cases, they also have a research background to facilitate their interaction with the research community. All of our examples come from large, research-intensive universities, which have more than 10 people providing centralised Research Data Management (RDM) support in addition to these domain-specific consultants.

## 'Show Me the Money'

One differentiating factor among the three cases is the business model. While both TU Delft and Virginia Tech pay for the salaries of their domain consultants from faculty budgets, at Utrecht University the salary of data managers is covered by research grants. This has implications for the feasibility of implementation elsewhere. The TU Delft and Virginia Tech models are more challenging to implement, because of the need to allocate central budget for the positions. The Utrecht University model offers more flexibility and scalability: the greater the demand, the more projects ask for data management support, and the more money becomes available to hire data managers.

All three cases have slightly different flavours and twists to them. So without any further spoilers, enjoy our three picks!

# 6.1. Data Stewards at TU Delft: A Reality Check for Disciplinary RDM

*Author: Yan Wang*

*Contributor: Alastair Dunning*

*TU Delft employs former researchers as Data Stewards within each faculty, creating a full-time local contact for RDM advice who engage with researchers and inform them about other institutional support services and resources.*

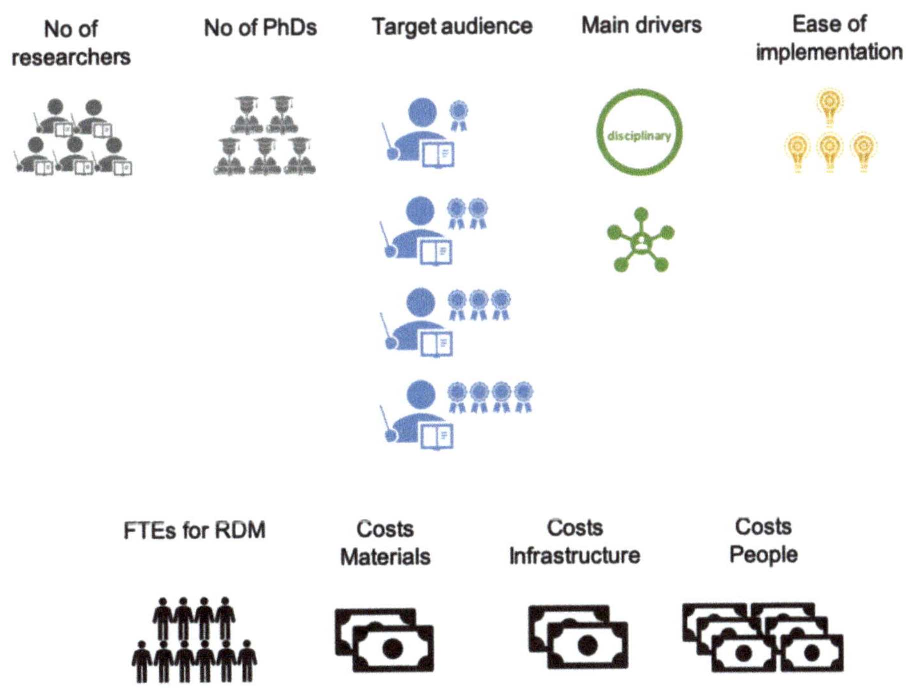


Table 6.1, CC BY 4.0.

 https://doi.org/10.11647/OBP.0185.18

Fostering cultural change is the objective of the Data Stewardship program. Delft University of Technology (TU Delft) in the Netherlands were bold: they hired 8 researchers to act as Data Stewards at each faculty. These are professional Research Data Management (RDM) specialists tasked with improving daily data management practices within their research communities. 'Our message is simple. If researchers have any questions about their research data, the Data Steward is their go-to person. Researchers are there to do research; they can't be expected to know everything about the latest tools available, or about all the nitty gritty details of policies and regulations. Data Stewards serve as bridges between the researchers and all other research support services, such as the library, ethics committee, ICT (Information, Communication and Technology), privacy and legal teams,' says Yan Wang, the Data Steward at the Faculty of Architecture and Built Environment. The daily job of the Data Steward is therefore to respond to researchers' requests, advise them, and promote good RDM practices.

## Job Definition: Have Disciplinary Expertise in Data Management, Take Initiative and Be a People Person

All Data Stewards are former researchers. They have a PhD degree, or equivalent experience to match the research background of the faculties they work for. This allows them to fit in with the faculty culture and develop discipline-specific data policies.

Being the only RDM person serving the entire faculty presents challenges. 'You need to take a lot of initiative to define the job, to reach out to people and make yourself visible. RDM is still a new subject, and it is challenging to help researchers, especially those who are not aware of the benefits of good RDM practices. The only way to raise awareness is to meet them, talk to them, get to know their work and make them understand what the benefits of good data management practices are,' explains Yan.

This is why Data Stewards need to have exceptional communication skills and enjoy working with people. 'Interpersonal skills are key to the success of the Data Steward,' reflects Alastair Dunning, the Head of Research Data Services at TU Delft. Alastair was one of the founders of the Data Stewardship programme. 'Once we connect with researchers, the interactions are typically very positive and allow development of strong relationships and incremental improvement of data management practices,' adds Yan.

Fig. 6.1 Software carpentry workshop organized by Data Stewards. © Yan Wang / TU Delft, CC BY 4.0.

## Coordination Is Crucial to Create Operational Synergy

Data Stewards are embedded in faculties and centrally coordinated by the library-based Data Stewardship Coordinator. In order to provide comprehensive research support, operational synergy among all support teams at the university is paramount. Good RDM practices put new requirements on the workflows where different teams are involved. The Data Stewardship Coordinator plays an important role in bringing the different teams together. The Coordinator constantly steers the communication and facilitates joint efforts.

## Institutional Support Is Needed for Implementation

In response to emerging trends, new positions are needed at research institutions. This is not a common practice, and needs support from senior management willing to take risks and provide adequate investment to allow innovations and developments. 'Perhaps we should focus not so much on having the perfect technical infrastructure, but on whether we have the right people. People are key drivers of cultural change and that's the essence of our data stewardship initiative,' concludes Alastair.

# 6.2. Cultural Change Happens One Person at a Time: Informatics Lab at Virginia Tech

*Author: Marta Teperek*
*Contributor: Jonathan Petters*

***Virginia Tech employs researcher-consultants to provide expert support within specific domains and build good practice through ongoing partnerships with researchers.***

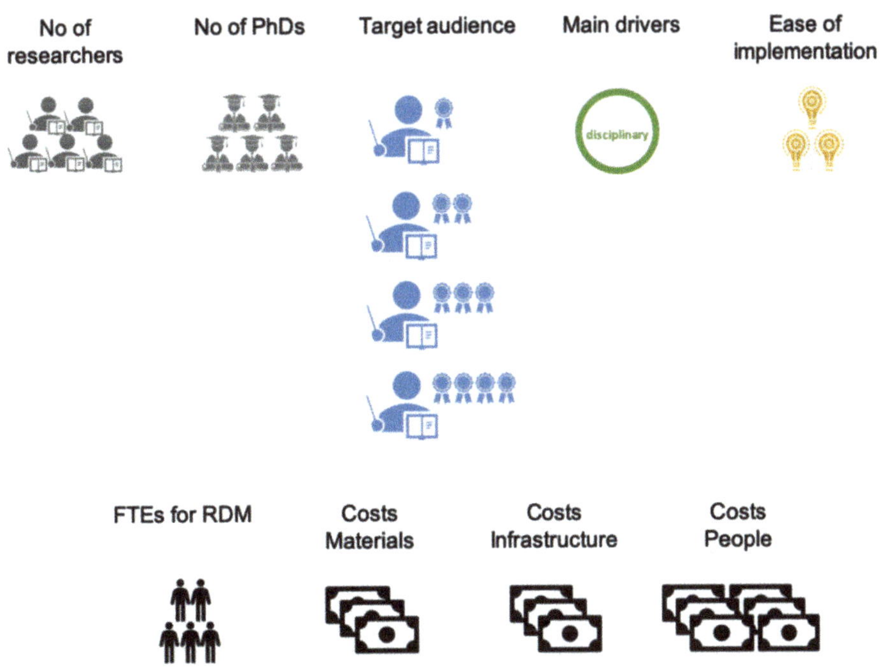


Table 6.2, CC BY 4.0.

 https://doi.org/10.11647/OBP.0185.19

'To a large extent, researchers are not interested in data management planning. Apart from the fact that they have to do it for grant proposals, they're generally not interested in sharing data. They want their problems to be solved: "my workflow is really inefficient and I wish it were better", or, "I would really love to use this new software, but I can't figure out how to get it to work". So our aim with the Informatics Lab is to help researchers where they want help. While helping them we have the opportunity to talk to them about data management planning and data sharing,' explains Jonathan Petters, Data Management Consultant and Curation Services Coordinator at Virginia Tech.

Fig. 6.2.1 Jonathan Petters, Data Management Consultant and Curation Services Coordinator at Virginia Tech © Jonathan Petters, CC BY 4.0.

## Domain-Specific Consultants at the Informatics Lab

The Informatics Lab was established as part of the Data Services unit with the goal of helping researchers across all disciplines to deal efficiently with their data. The team consists of five people: four consultants and one coordinator.[1] All consultants have domain knowledge to help them

1 Informatics Lab at Virginia Tech, https://informaticslab.lib.vt.edu/

develop deeper interactions and relationships with researchers. 'Finding the right person for the position is a challenge,' says Jonathan. 'You need people who have a good understanding of the research lifecycle and of data management, but also the ability to think at a higher level than just one research project. You want a combination of both depth and a higher, broader view.'

Jonathan also explains that in addition to all the research requirements, it is crucial for the consultants to have a genuine interest in offering support: 'If you're not interested in helping out other people, you're not the right person. A good way to test this is to make sure that people to which the services will be provided are involved in the hiring committee.'

## Research Background — A Double-Edged Sword?

The informatics consultants are employed as permanent faculty members, meaning that they are researchers in their own right. They are expected to maintain a research portfolio and to publish. 'Actively doing research is not in direct opposition to being a good service provider, but I think that there's a bit of tension. Some of our consultants feel they are here to help. Others focus more on their research and do some consultancy on the side,' reflects Jonathan. 'But the benefit is that by doing their own research, it's even easier for them to get out and talk to other researchers. They form organic networks through shared interests and connections, and that's how mutual awareness and trust is created. I could talk to a biomedical researcher about human subjects' data because I know these issues pretty well. But if I say that my background is meteorology, they may say, okay, so you know something about research, but that's from a different domain. Having somebody who's got that background brings credence.'

## Five Full-Time Employees Are Expensive — Are They Worth the Investment?

The group has had over 200 consultations so far. They have a big body of evidence that they will eventually look into, but Jonathan prefers not to rely solely on quantitative feedback: 'Everybody was saying

Fig. 6.2.2 Informatics Lab at work. © Ann Brown/Virginia Tech, CC BY 4.0.2.

they were really happy. So unless people are willing to be upfront and critical with you, you're not likely to receive helpful feedback. Nobody is going to say: "I know you tried to help me for 6 hours, but in fact you made it worse".' Jonathan prefers to focus on long-term effects. 'When our consultants talk to researchers about the kind of data they produce, about all those different proteins and complex molecules, for example, they help researchers realise that it's actually all data. They get them to think about their research in a different way. This opens up an opportunity to have a conversation about changing their practice.' Jonathan reflects that when they help a researcher, they get a recurring client who views the library as a partner. 'It's a one person to one person thing and it leads to slow cultural change. We also help research students and that's going to have an impact on them moving forward. Whether they are all going to become tenure-track professors or not, it does contribute to cultural change.'

2 Virginia Tech News, 'University Libraries Has Expertise, Resources to Help Faculty Overcome Data Challenges', where the photo was originally published, https://vtnews.vt.edu/articles/2019/05/univlib-datasalvage-miller.html

# 6.3. Ever Heard of Five-Legged Sheep? Data Managers at Utrecht University Give Researchers a Leg-Up!

*Author: Iza Witkowska*
*Contributor: Martine Pronk*

***Utrecht University employs a pool of data managers who can be flexibly hired and embedded within research teams for short or long periods, providing highly targeted RDM support and allowing researchers to concentrate on research.***

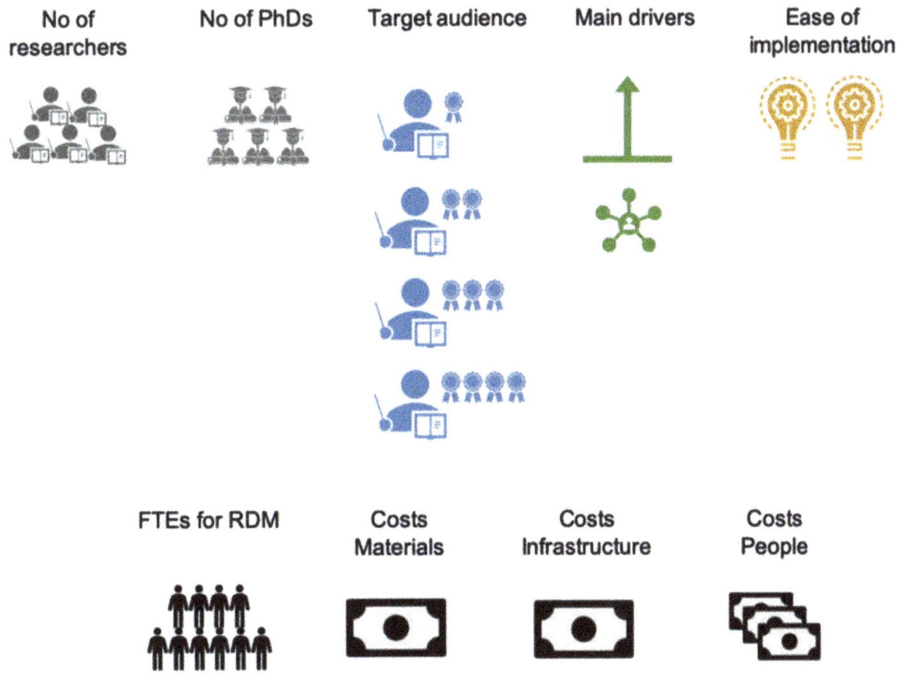


Table 6.3, CC BY 4.0.

 https://doi.org/10.11647/OBP.0185.20

'Demands in the various phases of the data cycle are so diverse that finding all expertise in one person is comparable to searching for the proverbial "five-legged sheep",' says Martine Pronk, the head of Academic Services of the Utrecht University (UU) Library.

The 'five-legged sheep' is an old Dutch expression, referring to somebody who needs to be unreasonably versatile. And sadly, this is what is expected from the twenty-first-century researcher.[3] Transparent and well-documented data management is one of many tasks that researchers now need to add to their already heavy workload.

The UU flexible data managers' pool takes the technical aspects of managing data away from overwhelmed researchers. A data manager can be hired from the library and embedded in a research project part-time or full-time, either short-term for small, specific tasks, such as support in writing a data management plan, or for longer periods, for example to set up a data flow and help to manage the data collection over an entire project. In this way, expertise that is developed stays within the university, in contrast to the scenario of hiring an external (and most likely expensive) expert for the same job.

At UU the data manager service was set up in response to a request for expertise. In 2017 the program director of an ongoing large-scale study with multiple partners, the YOUth cohort study,[4] requested a skilled professional to help with managing data. The library responded enthusiastically to this request and the service of the embedded data manager was born. Reflecting on the success of this project, it was expected that more of these projects would be initiated at the UU (and elsewhere). The popularity of this service has since increased and it has been promoted as vital by satisfied customers[5] to their peers.

'The data managers' pool fits well in the traditional values of the library to make research output findable, available, accessible and re-usable. What's new is that in response to the changing needs of the scientific community and digital innovations, the library and its employees move closer to the researchers,' says Martine.

---

3 'Reflections on Research Assessment for Researcher Recruitment and Career Progression — talking while acting? ' (blog post), https://openworking.wordpress.com/2019/05/20/reflections-on-research-assessment-for-researcher-recruitment-and-career-progression-talking-while-acting/

4 YOUth Cohort Study, https://www.uu.nl/en/research/youth-cohort-study/youth

5 Interview with Prof. Chantal Kemner, 24 June 2019, https://www.uu.nl/en/news/mapping-the-territory-of-child-development-with-team-science

The best way to start this service is by having large, data-driven, complex projects or programmes with multiple (inter)national stakeholders. These projects are more likely to have enough funding and to require high quality data management support to manage all the data flows. It also helps to have a well-developed Research Data Management (RDM) network within the university to promote the service among the researchers and help identify researchers and projects that could benefit from it.

## The Secret Ingredients Are People

The perfect candidate for the role of data manager should be someone who is able to act as an advisor, project manager and leader, as well as contributing technical skills in RDM. He or she needs to be proactive, flexible, show initiative and be able to work effectively within, and contribute to, a positive team environment. They also need to be capable of building productive networks both internally and externally. And of course, they need to have both passion and experience with managing data and the ability to communicate their expertise to others.

For data managers, having a PhD might be helpful to understand the research environment, but is not required. What is necessary is the ability to communicate effectively with researchers. Because this function is new and the field of data management is dynamic, data managers have a unique opportunity to develop and customize their role according to the needs of the scientific community and their own professional interests.

The main challenge for the service is acquiring new projects and doing so in a timely manner, in order to have enough projects on the go at any given time. The pool and individual data managers have targets and they need to meet them: currently 65% of the collective FTEs (Full-Time Equivalents) need to be outsourced to projects. To achieve this goal, data managers need to look continuously for projects and use their networks to increase the visibility of the service.

Although it's a relatively new service, there are two clear indicators showing that this service is well received by the scientific community and promotes good data management practices. 'Firstly, interest, demand and appreciation for this service is growing, and researchers themselves promote this service to their colleagues. Secondly, data managers act

Fig. 6.3 Data managers Ron Scholten and Danny de Koning at the KinderKennisCentrum of Utrecht University. 

as ambassadors of FAIR (Findable, Accessible, Interoperable, Re-usable) and open data. They educate and advise researchers on good data management practices, including how to archive or publish data and metadata standards. More and more datasets get published at the UU,' says Martine.

RDM
Annemiek
Anneke
Universiteit
Utrecht
University
good
can
story
stories
says
data
researcher
interview
Vrije
activity
network
subject
practices
profile
raise
write
share
similar
talk
also
peers
two
teams
engagement
Kuil
der
van
Maat
Research
Researchers
visibility
promote
services
convinced
helped
identify
experience
increasing
norms
interviewed
officer
members
practice
better
David
like
see
way
just
even
time
use
take
ask
work
start
Need
Support
believe
convince
tools
need
certain
know
Data
right
one
Table
best
well

# 7. Interviews and Case Studies

Research Data Management (RDM) professionals, librarians, funders and even university boards around the globe are convinced that good data management practices benefit researchers and science. But what do the researchers have to say about this?

At two Dutch universities, RDM teams took the initiative to go and ask. As a result, they didn't only successfully engage with the scientific community, but they also helped researchers to raise their professional profile, to act as RDM ambassadors and to promote good data management to their peers.

Both teams agree that it turned out to be an effective way of increasing the visibility of RDM teams and their services. As they also approached this activity in a similar way ('just go and do it'), used similar resources (that is, by employing a communication advisor/officer), and have 'similar lessons to share with you', we decided to present these two cases together.

# 7.1. Showcasing Peers and their Good Practice: Researcher Interviews at Vrije Universiteit Amsterdam and Utrecht University

*Author: Iza Witkowska*

*Contributor: Annemiek van der Kuil and Anneke de Maat*

***Staff at Vrije Universiteit Amsterdam and Utrecht University interview researchers whose stories illustrate the value of good RDM, to provide peer-driven examples of good practice and raise the profile of exemplary researchers.***

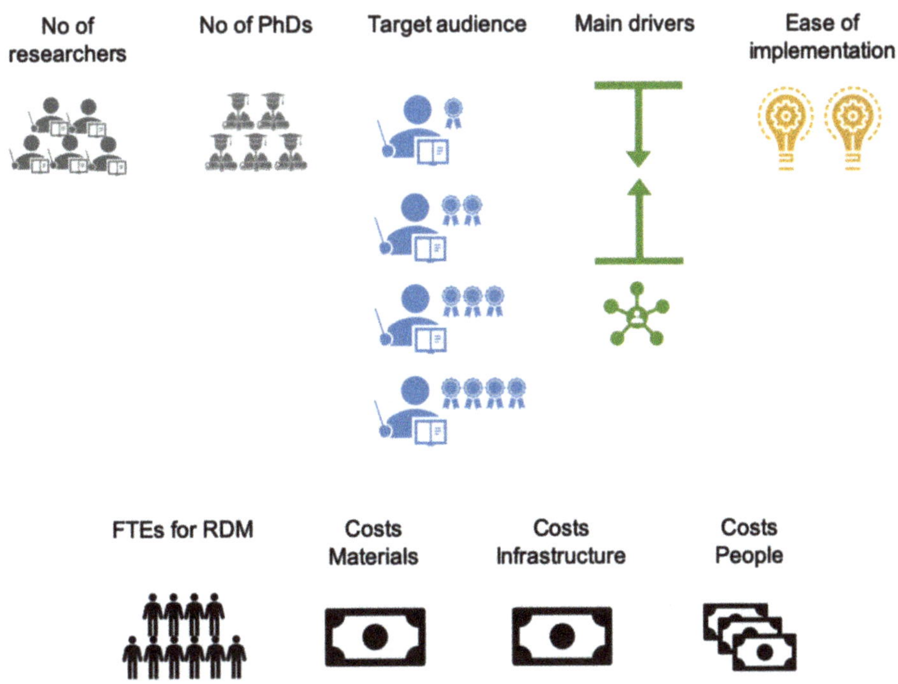


Table 7.1.1 Utrecht University, CC BY 4.0.

 https://doi.org/10.11647/OBP.0185.21

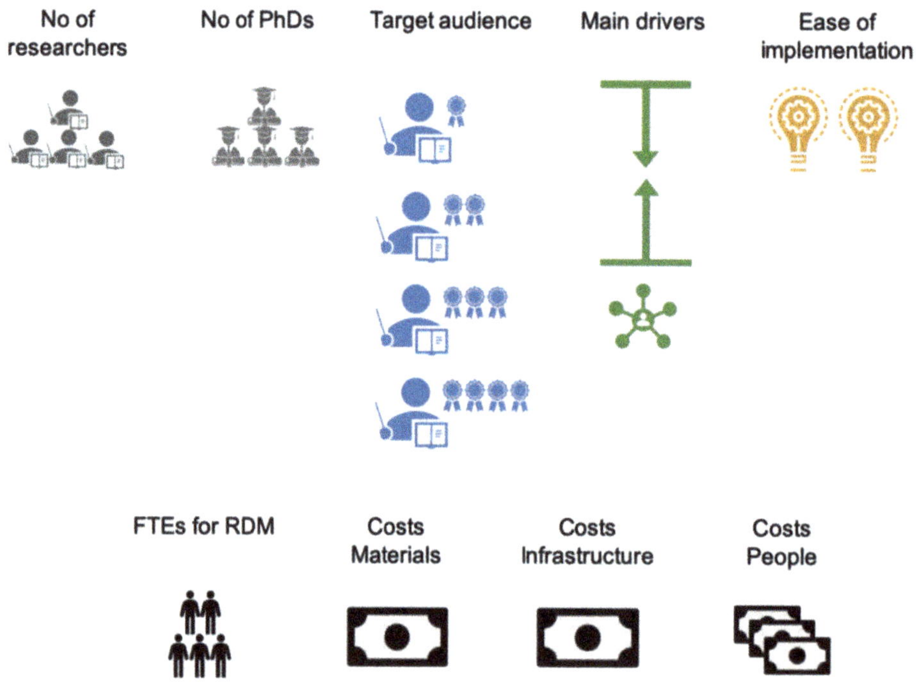


Table 7.1.2 Vrije Universiteit Amsterdam, CC BY 4.0.

*If you would convince a man that he does wrong, do right. But do not care to convince him. Men will believe what they see. Let them see. —* ***Henry David Thoreau***

If you want to promote good data management practice, do this by highlighting the work of those researchers who lead by example. Tell their stories and showcase why and how good Research Data Management (RDM) helped them to achieve their goals. 'People are more convinced by the information which is given by their peers. Social norms govern the behaviour of members of a society. When researchers see that other researchers from their peer group use certain tools or services, they are more likely to start using these tools and services,' says Anneke de Maat, the communication advisor at the Vrije Universiteit Amsterdam (VU).

Interviewing people is a fun and interesting activity. You get an opportunity to get to know the person with whom you are talking, and the subject about which they are passionate. 'Researchers do like to talk. They like to talk about their research experiences and beyond; about their success stories and frustrations,' explains Annemiek van der Kuil, the RDM consultant at the Utrecht University (UU). 'They feel flattered and take this as an opportunity to raise their professional profile,' adds Anneke. Annemiek's and Anneke's advice is that you 'just go and try' interviewing as a form of engagement!

Both Vrije Universiteit Amsterdam[1] and Utrecht University[2] write up and share their interviews online, and archive them for future reference. Interviews are conducted with researchers at all stages, from PhD students to senior academics, and cover topics such as disciplinary norms, use of specific software, and best practices for managing certain kinds of data.

## What Ingredients Do You Need to Get Started?

**Ingredient one**: an excellent communications officer or a member of your team who can approach a researcher and ask the right questions.

**Ingredient two**: a dedicated colleague, or even better, a network of colleagues, who work closely with researchers and are able to identify interesting case studies. 'At the UU, members of the RDM network are our best friends and ambassadors!' says Annemiek.

**Ingredient three**: good fortune on your side, so that the identified researcher is willing to participate. Even better, if you can identify an influential researcher with a catchy subject and their own broad network, then the story can go viral after its publication. 'At the UU, we were lucky to interview "Mr. Drought" [Niko Wanders], the national expert on drought!'[3]

**Ingredient four**: someone who can take good photos. 'It gives this extra touch to the whole experience and researchers definitely like it!' says Annemiek.

1 Archive of the VU newsletter with all interviews, https://ub.vu.nl/en/news-agenda/vu-research-support-newsletter/archive/index.aspx

2 Interviews with researchers at Utrecht University, https://www.uu.nl/en/research/research-data-management/rdm-stories

3 Interview with Niko Wanders, 7 February 2019, https://www.uu.nl/en/background/in-our-research-community-data-sharing-is-the-norm

**Ingredient five**: a good story: 'a story which is as personal and honest as possible; one that draws a realistic picture and provides concrete and practical information to the reader,' says Anneke.

**Ingredient six**: have, or create, communication channels to distribute your message.

Need more tips and tricks? Here they come: (1) prepare for the interview by researching the subject and the interviewee; (2) conduct the interview on your own; (3) be as objective and open-minded as you can — try to withhold any judgement over what the interviewee tells you; (4) let the researcher talk; and, (5) write your story with enthusiasm and with the interest of your audience at heart.

Fig. 7.1 Elise Quik at the David de Wied Building of the Faculty of Science, Utrecht University. © Annemiek van der Kuil | PhotoA.nl, all rights reserved.

It's not all 'butterflies and rainbows'; this activity can be time consuming. 'It takes 6 to 7 working hours to do the interview, write and edit a story,' says Anneke. Hiring an external communication officer can be expensive. Moreover, researchers at VU have busy agendas, need to prioritize tasks and might not have time to be interviewed. Identifying new stories and making sure that your story reaches the right ears gets easier with experience and as your network grows, but can be challenging to start with.

How do we know that this activity creates engagement and promotes our cause? 'At the UU, more and more researchers find their way to our RDM Support Office. We believe it's not only because of the growing need for the RDM Support, but also thanks to our increasing visibility,' says Annemiek. 'We haven't had a researcher refusing our invitation to be interviewed. Researchers, as well as their peers, are happy to share RDM stories and, at the end, researchers learn from each other about good data management practices,' conclude both Anneke and Annemiek. This is called 'a job well done'!

data
Data
digital
Research
Seniors
HBS
can
time
RDM
career
library
Stein
UiT
senior
role
practices
make
Arctic
legacy
new
one
many
others
help
within
forms
leave
talk
preserve
organise
key
use
School
similar
means
formats
driver
transition
case
share
like
first
feel
etc
well
it's
starts
Table
Wise
open
learn
files
Elli
adapted
different
often
able
retires
needed
especially
part
services
McNeill
Author
familiar
need
shift
lost
End
long
access
program
dataset
storing
plans
rarely
order
Start
idea
will
datasets
groups
subject
archive
meetings
expected
always
assistants

# 8. Engage with Senior Researchers through Archiving

We are all familiar with what a data management lifecycle looks like: you start with the idea or the concept for your research journey, then move on to collecting a dataset and analysing it, then cleaning and tidying it up to prepare it for sharing, before finally preserving or archiving it for perpetuity. That is the ideal Research Data Management (RDM) scenario, but most of the time the final archiving step never happens. Instead, data remains with the original researchers and moves around with them. 'What if the researcher retires or dies?' you might ask. Well, often the dataset is lost, unless a colleague can find it and bring it to their institution for preservation, which is rarely the case. Researchers may be familiar with the idea of donating books, papers and special collections, but rarely think of their messy draft documents, data from unpublished research projects, or password-protected USB sticks and hard drives.

## A Turnaround in Habit

In the world of open science, where the reproducibility of research is of increasing concern, some institutional archives have become a key driver of cultural change and good RDM practices. Archives are typically responsible for persistently securing and preserving the intellectual legacy of the institutions they serve, and this role requires engagement from those who create this content.

In order to understand how some archives have managed to successfully communicate their role in RDM within their institutions, we present two case studies: the Harvard Business School Archives (USA),[1] and the UiT The Arctic University of Norway Library (Norway).[2] These case studies reflect their institutional settings, and provide interesting approaches to managing research data.

1 Harvard Business School Archives, https://www.library.hbs.edu/Services/Baker-Library-Services/Archives-Records-Management

2 UiT The Arctic University of Norway Library, https://en.uit.no/ub

# 8.1. Soliciting Deposit and Preservation of University-Produced Research Data as Part of Broader Archives and Records Management Work

*Author: Elli Papadopoulou*

*Contributor: Katherine McNeill and Rachel Wise*

***Staff from the Harvard Business School (HBS) Archives share their views on how the transition from physical to digital management practices helps engage with researchers who are about to leave the institution.***

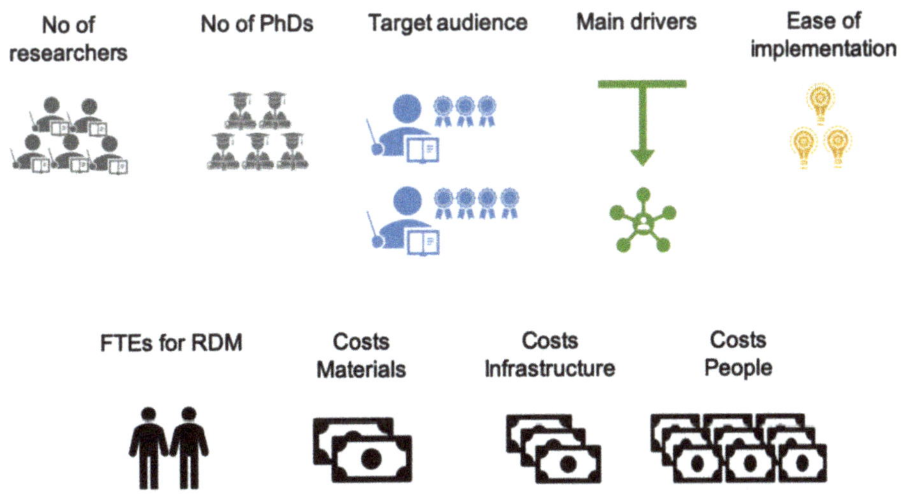


Table 8.1, CC BY 4.0.[1]

1 Note that the figures above are for Harvard Business School and not for Harvard University overall.

 https://doi.org/10.11647/OBP.0185.22

## Don't Forget about the Physical Data!

You might think that research data management is a recent trend resulting from funders' requirements for open and FAIR (Findable, Accessible, Interoperable, Re-usable), machine-actionable data. But is that the only driver? Katherine McNeill, Research Data Program Manager, explains the role of the Harvard Business School (HBS) Archives: 'Since the early twentieth century, the HBS Archives have been preserving the data produced by the School's faculty as part of its mission to preserve its research in all forms. Activities include a proactive program of data collection, as well as a storage service for post-project research records.' She points out that 'many organisations have an opportunity to collect research data by leveraging programs that already exist to actively preserve institutional records.'

Their key message from this long history of curation is that, despite current discussions about big data and digital disruption, data are not always in a digital form and archives have experience of looking after physical data that can also be applied to digital data. Rachel Wise, HBS Archivist, explains that the Archives have a tradition of curating and storing paper forms of research data, including notes, physical articles and other published papers, survey data, agreements, consent forms, accepted proposals, correspondence, etc. The steps followed for physical research records are not drastically different to managing digital data: researchers first hand over the data collected during their research and an archivist works with them to clean up and curate the data, and to decide what to keep for the long term.

## It's about Shifting Perspectives

Of course there are as many challenges when dealing with physical data management, as there are for digital asset management, and some are similar in nature, but the HBS Archives prefer to look at challenges as opportunities to grow. The importance of integrating electronic data management procedures into existing workflows is one challenge shared with physical data management, along with having the infrastructure to carry out the necessary actions for that data management; such activities necessitate expanding the archive's partnerships with research computing services to better facilitate the transition between the active phase of research and the long-term data management.

For the HBS Archives, developing infrastructure from scratch is not necessary, as they already make use of the university's repository for web-based publishing of research data. However, they are working on improving their local IT (Information Technology) infrastructure for medium-term storage of digital files to help faculty members retain research data until they are ready to share or archive their data. This is the same service the HBS Archives have provided to faculty members for physical records for decades, adapted to address digital data.

Finally, many HBS researchers are not subject to producing funder-required data management plans, whether for physical or digital data, and thus miss an opportunity to plan responsible and reproducible research practices from the beginning of a project.

## What the Future Holds

Katherine and Rachel both highlight the need to be more proactive, and to continuously develop and expand the archive service so that digital data can be effectively curated in the archives. Rachel continues: 'Now the approach is more reactive: when someone reaches out to us before a career shift or retirement, we are there to support them by providing guidance and physical storage; this could be for a researcher at any level of their career'. Being more proactive means cultivating researchers' mind-sets so that they are willing to organise and prepare data for sharing before they leave the institution, or prior to the end of their project; it means exploring the best ways to reach out to faculty members, and it means applying technical solutions that will facilitate digital data-sharing of valuable research assets.

## Confused about Where to Start? Foster Data Champions and Build upon Existing Services

Both Katherine and Rachel agree that one of the top priorities when establishing an engagement activity is raising awareness and educating researchers about what you can do. 'You have to be able to talk to people in a language that they understand. And who better to take on that role than researchers themselves? So it is wise to encourage faculty users of the service to educate their peers. Having a faculty champion, who can talk about how much their data has been re-used because of your services, can go a long way in promoting your research data management program,' they state.

There is an opportunity to partner with, and leverage, your institutional archives to preserve research data since they are already set up as a service provider and repository for institutional records. Archives have policies, procedures and relationships in place, which can be extended to organise, store and provide access to research data in all formats.

# 8.2. Starting at the End: Seniors' Research Data Project at the UiT The Arctic University of Norway

*Author: Elli Papadopoulou*

*Contributors: Stein Høydalsvik, Leif Longva*

***The Library of UiT, The Arctic University of Norway, gives insight into their Seniors' Research Data project and walk us through the links and networks established so far, and all of their achievements to date.***

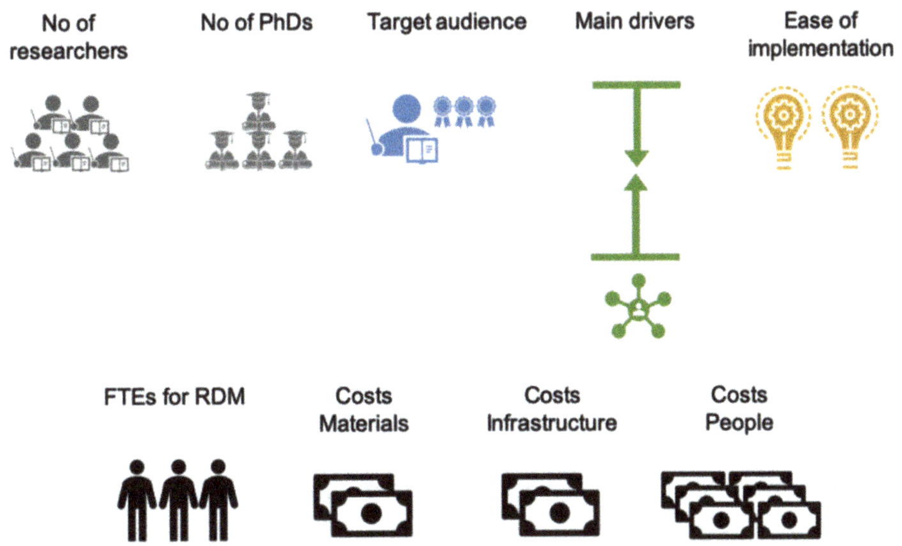


Table 8.2, CC BY 4.0.

 https://doi.org/10.11647/OBP.0185.23

## What If You Start at the End?

What happens to data once a researcher retires? According to Lars Figenschou, from the Library of UiT The Arctic University of Norway, 'there is empirical evidence that the data collected by researchers who are leaving research are those most at risk of being lost. This is a huge problem for the research community, as well as for the institutions.' Stein Høydalsvik, senior advisor at the library, clarifies that the main driver of their project is re-usability: 'We need to be able to access and re-use data that have been generated within our institution; it's equally a matter of preserving the legacy and of enabling others to make something new out of it.'

The goal of the Seniors' Research Data project is to identify the most valuable datasets created by senior researchers. The library is responsible for curating data (reviewing the submitted data and communicating with the submitting researcher on how to present the data through good metadata and descriptions, and on recommended file-format conversions, etc.), while the faculty is expected to help researchers select the most valuable datasets and advise them on the most suitable, discipline-appropriate data management practices.

One of the UiT faculties supported the project by allocating money to fund research assistants to help their senior researchers prepare their data for archiving, for example, by digitising, structuring and describing the data. However, not many researchers made use of this funding. The reason appeared to be that, even with funded assistants, researchers themselves still needed to prepare their research data materials for archiving. A major obstacle to the success of a project like the Seniors' Research Data project is the fact that research data archiving, especially of old data, requires time and effort by the researchers.

## How Do Senior Researchers Differ from Early-Career Researchers?

It is sometimes thought that acquiring a new skill gets harder with age, but in Stein's experience the most important factor is the willingness of individuals to learn new things. The impression in the Research Data Management (RDM) team at UiT is that senior researchers are more motivated to secure their research legacy than researchers in earlier stages of their careers. Senior researchers, especially those about to retire, seem quite willing to learn how to adequately prepare their data for sharing, perhaps because they feel less competitive as their career is established and because they have no further plans to use the data for their own research.

A similar effect is observed when reaching out to researchers who are about to make a career shift, and who rely on the library archives for storing and preserving their data. However, Stein warns that researchers at this stage often hold the messiest data. Perhaps this is to be expected given that senior researchers have been collecting data for longer: years of modifying documents, creating new versions and formats of the same files, using the same file names on multiple occasions, and similar issues can lead to data chaos when compounded over time.

## Targeting the Right People

Here is where support from the library, with its strong networks and collaborations, comes in handy. Stein explains how they have adapted the library's RDM support workflows to fit the Seniors' Research Data project.

It starts with effective communication from the Library Director, which then cascades down to the Deans of Faculties, Heads of Departments, and then to Principal Investigators and individual research groups. Next, an RDM specialist from the library usually starts by arranging meetings on different levels within the faculty: first with the Dean and key personnel to inform them about the Seniors' Researcher Data project, then meeting with research groups and faculty to discuss what is needed from their side.

If there is interest, the archivists organise hands-on sessions and provide detailed guidelines, sometimes with one-to-one conversations and meetings, as appropriate.

## Coming Out of Your Comfort Zone: A Tough Decision

Stein explains that the success of the Seniors' Research Data project crucially depends on staff, for example, on subject librarians willing to leave their desk and having the courage to approach and cooperate with researchers on a topic that they don't necessarily feel comfortable with. However, Stein says that, 'it's not the specific role or job title that librarians have that will make a difference, but their attitude. Knowing the RDM policy landscape is one thing, but in order to be heard, you have to go where the researchers are and talk to them in a language that they understand.'

Fig. 8.2 Prof Robert T. Barrett collecting data about seabirds and migratory birds. Retired in 2018 after 40 years of work at the UiT. © Adrien Brun, CC BY 4.0.

Prof Robert T. Barrett reflects on the selfish benefits of archiving his data: 'It's just positive and fun if my time series data can benefit others. And extra nice if they refer to me. I get a quote, and at the same time others know that I actually collected the data.'

However, the benefits go far beyond merely selfish reasons: 'as a researcher, one can always make excuses about lack of time, but we actually have a moral duty: what we have published is only part of the legacy. We should be proud enough of what we have done during our research career to make all our data and research materials publicly available, for the benefit of younger researchers and all our successors.'

# Contributors

## Editors

**Connie Clare**, TU Delft, The Netherlands, 0000-0002-4369-196X

**Maria Cruz**, VU Amsterdam, The Netherlands, 0000-0001-9111-182X

**James Savage**, University of Cambridge / University of Sheffield, The United Kingdom, 0000-0002-4737-5673

**Joanne Yeomans**, Leiden University, The Netherlands 0000-0002-0738-7661

## Authors

**Connie Clare**, TU Delft, The Netherlands, 0000-0002-4369-196X

**Elli Papadopoulou**, Athena Research Center, Greece / OpenAIRE, 0000-0002-0893-8509

**Marta Teperek**, TU Delft, The Netherlands, 0000-0001-8520-5598

**Yan Wang**, TU Delft, The Netherlands, 0000-0002-6317-7546

**Iza Witkowska**, Utrecht University, The Netherlands

**Joanne Yeomans**, Leiden University, The Netherlands 0000-0002-0738-7661

## Illustrators

**Connie Clare**, TU Delft, The Netherlands, 0000-0002-4369-196X

**Elli Papadopoulou**, Athena Research Center, Greece / OpenAIRE, 0000-0002-0893-8509

**Yan Wang**, TU Delft, The Netherlands, 0000-0002-6317-7546

**Iza Witkowska**, Utrecht University, The Netherlands

## Case-Study Contributors

**Helene N. Andreassen**, UiT The Arctic University of Norway, Norway, 0000-0001-9450-803X

**Lauren Cadwallader**, University of Cambridge, The United Kingdom, 0000-0002-7571-3502

**Dan Crane**, King's College London, The United Kingdom, 0000-0002-7197-0974

**Maria Cruz**, VU Amsterdam, The Netherlands, 0000-0001-9111-182X

**Alastair Dunning**, Delft University of Technology, The Netherlands 0000-0002-8344-4883

**Christopher Gibson**, The University of Manchester, The United Kingdom, 0000-0002-1880-3755

**Ramutė Grabauskienė**, Vilnius University, Lithuania

**Mary-Kate Hannah**, University of Glasgow, The United Kingdom, 0000-0001-7777-0140

**Rosie Higman**, The University of Manchester (to July 2019), The United Kingdom, 0000-0001-5329-7168

**Annemarie Hildegard Eckes-Shephard**, University of Cambridge, The United Kingdom, 0000-0002-2453-3843

**Stein Høydalsvik**, UiT The Arctic University of Norway, Norway

**Sacha Jones**, University of Cambridge, The United Kingdom, 0000-0003-0492-2662

**Annemiek van der Kuil**, Utrecht University, The Netherlands

**Wendy Liu**, University of Technology Sydney, Australia

**Leif Longva**, UiT The Arctic University of Norway, Norway

**Duncan Loxton**, University of Technology Sydney, Australia

**Anneke de Maat**, Vrije Universiteit Amsterdam, The Netherlands

**Kerry Miller**, University of Edinburgh, The United Kingdom

**Alicia Hofelich Mohr**, University of Minnesota, The United States of America 0000-0002-7644-4105

**Jenny McBurney**, University of Minnesota, The United States of America, 0000-0003-4081-6066

**Katherine McNeill**, Harvard Business School, The United States of America

**Jonathan Petters**, Virginia Tech University Libraries, The United States of America 0000-0002-0853-5814

**Martine Pronk**, Utrecht University, The Netherlands

**James Savage**, University of Cambridge / University of Sheffield, The United Kingdom, 0000-0002-4737-5673

**Hardy Schwamm**, National University of Ireland Galway, Ireland, 0000-0003-1325-5259

**Fieke Schoots**, Leiden University, The Netherlands 0000-0002-4385-9312

**Joshua Sendall**, Lancaster University, The United Kingdom 0000-0002-2057-4912

**Laurents Sesink**, Leiden University, The Netherlands 0000-0001-7880-5413

**Joseph Ssebulime**, Makerere University, Uganda 0000-0002-9411-1515

**Elizabeth Stokes**, University of Technology Sydney, Australia

**Yasemin Türkyilmaz-van der Velden**, Delft University of Technology, The Netherlands, 0000-0003-2562-0452

**Erik van den Bergh**, Wageningen University and Research, The Netherlands, 0000-0001-9865-574X

**Saskia van Marrewijk**, Wageningen University and Research, The Netherlands, 0000-0002-4630-630X

**Rachel Wise**, Harvard Business School, The United States of America

**Sharyn Wise**, University of Technology Sydney, Australia

## Project Members

Helene N. Andreassen, Szymon Andrzejewski, Daniel Bangert, Miriam Braskova, Grzegorz Bulczak, Lauren Cadwallader, John Chodacki, Julien Colomb, Philipp Conzett, Maria Cruz, Mary Donaldson, Biswanath Dutta, Esther Fernandez, Joshua Finnell, Raman Ganguly, Lambert Heller, Patricia Henning, Rosie Higman, Amy Hodge, Stein Høydalsvik, Greg Janée, Lynda Kellam, Gabor Kismihok, Iryna Kuchma, Narendra Kumar Bhoi, Young-Joo Lee, Leif Longva, Andrea Medina-Smith, Solomon Mekonnen, Remedios Melero, Rising Osazuwa, Elli Papadopoulou, Fernanda Peset, Josiline Chigwada, Vanessa Proudman, Piyachat Ratana, Gerry Ryder, James Savage, Souleymane Sogoba, Magdalena Szuflita-Żurawska, Ralf Toepfer, Ellen Verbakel, Irena Vipavc Brvar, Jacquelynne Waldron, Anna Wałek, Yan Wang, Iza Witkowska, Joanne Yeomans.

## Task Leaders

Julien Colomb, Maria Cruz, Raman Ganguly, Reme Melero, Marta Teperek, Iza Witkowska.

## Project Leader

Marta Teperek.

## Steering Board

Lauren Cadwallader, Julien Colomb, Maria Cruz, Mary Donaldson, Lambert Heller, Rosie Higman, Elli Papadopoulou, Vanessa Proudman, James Savage, Marta Teperek.

## The CRediT Roles

| Role | Definition | Contributors |
|---|---|---|
| Conceptualization | Ideas; formulation or evolution of overarching research goals and aims. | Project Leader<br>Steering Board<br>Task Leaders |
| Data Curation | Management activities to annotate (produce metadata), scrub data and maintain research data for initial use and later re-use. | Project Members |
| Funding acquisition | Acquisition of the financial support for the project leading to this publication. | Steering Board<br>Project Members |
| Investigation | Conducting a research and investigation process, specifically performing the experiments, or data/evidence collection. | Project Members<br>Case Study Contributors |
| Methodology | Development or design of methodology. | Project Members<br>Task Leaders<br>Steering Board |
| Project administration | Management and coordination responsibility for the research activity planning and execution. | Project Leader<br>Task Leaders |
| Resources | Provision of study materials, input information about research institutions and case study photographs. | Authors<br>Case Study Contributors<br>Project Members<br>Task Leaders |
| Supervision | Oversight and leadership responsibility for the research activity planning and execution, including mentorship external to the core team. | Project Leader<br>Task Leaders |
| Visualization | Preparation, creation and/or presentation of the published work, design and preparation of infographics to navigate through the book. | Illustrators<br>Editors |
| Writing — original draft | Preparation, creation and/or presentation of the published work, specifically writing the initial draft (including substantive translation). | Authors<br>Editors |

| Role | Definition | Contributors |
| --- | --- | --- |
| Writing — review & editing | Preparation, creation and/or presentation of the published work by those from the original research group, specifically critical review, commentary or revision — including pre- or post-publication stages. | Editors<br>Authors<br>Case Study Contributors |

# List of Illustrations and Tables

## Foreword



## Introduction



## Chapter 1

## Chapter 2



## Chapter 3

## Chapter 4



## Chapter 5



## Chapter 6

## Chapter 7



## Chapter 8

www.ingramcontent.com/pod-product-compliance
Lightning Source LLC
LaVergne TN
LVHW082235200926
848484LV00008B/2358